PORTRAIT OF A MARRIAGE

JUDY CRICHTON

Portrait of a Marriage

Bob Crichton at his Sunday softball game on Martha's Vineyard

He had been a writer. His novel, *The Secret of Santa Vittoria*, had been an enormous success and paid for this brownstone on the Upper West Side. He was the tall, ruddy man who everyone on the block knew, Big Bob who stepped out to chase muggers, help with cars that wouldn't start, play catch with the boys who lived next door. When he finally went away—Big Bob Crichton, the long ball hitter who quoted Yeats and Satchel Paige, the master of the Texas deadeye who carried an Arabic phrasebook in order to talk to the Yemenites who ran the candy store—when he finally shuffled off in a cloud of fear and confusion, a neighbor stopped me at the stoop to ask what had happened.

"I don't mean to pry," she said, "but we have all watched and wondered."

"He lost his mind," I said and went back into the house he called his big blue tomb.

His brain had been transformed into a neurological tangle with ascribed numbers none of us understood. The nurses at the VA hospital tried to lure him back to life in dance therapy in a pea-green room with fluorescent lights.

"What do you remember?" I asked. "Do you remember my name or the day that we married?"

"I remember the day we met," he said, "And I remember the War."

For months now I've been going through the cartons in the basement, through the papers in his office, through the diaries, manuscripts, letters, searching for what is left of his unfinished life. The medical reports are cruel but that doesn't mean they're accurate. The doctors are kind but not very scientific. No one reads what the last one wrote.

May 9, 1985
Medical Center Hospital of Vermont

Presenting Problem:
As I understand it, Mr. Crichton was
admitted to Spring Lake Ranch because of
alcoholism and self injurious behavior
aimed at ridding himself of the images of

the tombstones of the four young German
soldiers he shot during World War II.

When Bob left home for Spring Lake Ranch in
Vermont, his office looked as if it had been trashed in an
adolescent rage. Letters and unpaid bills mingled with
unfinished manuscripts. His heavy olive-green army coat
lay across the chair where he worked: a small chair with a
torn red-leatherette cushion and wrought-iron back that
he bought when we were first married. It was an absurd
chair for a six-foot-six man who could have afforded
better. Bob always was a tight man with a kopeck—as he
would say—even after he had written three bestsellers.

On the windowsill were chunks of coal brought back
from Scotland with a map of the mine where his great-
grandfather and uncles had worked tacked to the wall
above his typewriter. There were books and photographs,
boxes of clippings, pieces of shrapnel he had carried since
the Battle of the Bulge. Photographs of our children and
the perennially scowling Italian actress, Anna Magnani,
in costume on the *Santa Vittoria* set in Italy, old *Life*
magazines and his college copy of *The Oxford Book of
English Verse*, all scattered across the oak slab he used as
a desk.

There was the baseball bat so heavy the children
competed to try to swing it, a baseball with a smudged

autograph and, of course, the coal miner's pick he had brought back from Scotland when he was researching *The Camerons*, the novel inspired by his coal-mining family. The file cabinets had belonged to his father Kyle Crichton, also a writer, and held two generations of letters—yellowing scraps of paper from Hemingway and D.H. Lawrence to Kyle, Bob's exchanges with John Updike and Philip Roth, and our children's notes all jammed into one unsorted paper stew.

The office was painted blue—a bright dark blue. In his last years at home, Bob had become fixated on blue. One morning I left for work from our nice dark gray New York brownstone and returned in the evening to find it painted blue. At Christmas, Bob began to receive blue pitchers, blue ashtrays and blue coffee mugs from those who had never known what to give him. He had never wanted much.

Hidden under the stuff of his unfinished life were pages from two unfinished books he had talked so much about but none of us had seen. The book about the War was the one he had worked on the longest. It was now called *Memoirs of a Bad Soldier*. This was its preface:

Thirty years gone now since The War was ended.

I lie to myself, it is longer than that. I lie about
time these days. The years are beginning to skid
away like logs down a flume, each one distinguish-
able from the one that went before it, each one
equally forgotten. This distresses me because I
have come to believe in something Celine found
out: The greatest defeat, in anything, is to forget.
Forgetfulness dismantles time, the ultimate gift of
life. If something is forgotten, it never happened

and it is correct to say that loss of memory murders life.

Knowing this, I keep on forgetting. Days drift, it's always five o'clock in the afternoon, evening dropping down, too late to start anything, but still the swift slippage of the time of my life.

Failing to find any acceptable reason for this willful, even suicidal forgetfulness, I have come to blame it on the War. Because I remember the War.

I can't remember what I had for breakfast two mornings ago or where I might have been on this day two years ago but I can remember the meal I had on the morning of November 28, 1944. I can, with no effort at all, summon up the nostril-stinging mix of hot water and dark Barbados rum being poured into my metal canteen cup, meant to lend me courage and wash down the half-stale loaf of British bread someone clapped into my hand in the dawn darkness.

I could go to the stone barn where I had been sleeping and find the garden where I squatted later in the day, eating a can of American cheese and sucking lemon sour balls, staring across the black stalks and rain-swollen rutabagas, unharvested, at the bodies of two German soldiers lying in the leaves. One of them held a tin of Spanish sardines in his hand. I wanted them but I wouldn't pry them from his grip. Not from delicacy. I had gone beyond that by then, but because I was afraid of the transference of his death into me through the eating of the bodies of his fish. Death is catching.

I could, this minute, go to the drainage ditch where I was hiding at five o'clock that afternoon, alone in a sweep of beet fields that ran to the horizon like dark green swells of the sea, waiting for darkness to come and free me. I could, if pressed to do it, name every man in my outfit who died on this day.

Memory, then, is out of balance, the past is out of proportion. Sometimes, especially in winter when snow is in the fields, old images come back with such authority, the past luminous and magnified by time, whirring in my memory like an old newsreel, and it becomes hard for me to accept the present as the real and these lantern slides as the past and gone.

For a long time this didn't bother me because I couldn't see that this dominance by the past led to the paring down of the present. Nothing in the present ever seemed quite as compelling and real, nothing on such a grand scale as what had gone before. This I can see now resulted in a considerable loss of life, a muffling and muting of life, the present always diminished and disappointing by the excess of the past.

In this sense, I have come to see myself, along with many others of my time, as a casualty of war.

In the early days of our marriage, the War was a constant. Bob's army coat hung in the closet of our junk room along with his short jacket with its Purple Heart and the Railsplitters insignia of the 84th Infantry Division. Jagged shards of shrapnel rested on the kitchen shelf next to the wedding-present china. The War hovered over the table in the small French restaurant on Lexington Avenue where Bob first told me about the alter ego he sent into battle during the Battle of the Bulge while the real Bob Crichton cowered in a foxhole and waited for the shelling to end. He startled our waiter by blowing out the candles as he imitated the sound of incoming mortars. He described almost dying under friendly fire—the helplessness and absurdity of being bombarded by American planes. He tried to quantify fear and exhaustion, and I began to understand how much I could never understand.

Lying on his back in a meadow overlooking his parents' house in Connecticut, near the shack where he tried to raise chickens after college, Bob spoke more about that other self who leapt out of trenches and did all that the army expected while the real Bob Crichton used every trick he knew to stay alive. He told me about throwing away his rifle and carrying a shovel instead.

"Is that true?" I asked.

"I don't know," he said.

He talked about his feet, his frozen feet which almost rotted in the Battle of the Bulge during the cold and miserable Christmas of 1944. He talked about guilt and cowardice, about standing patrol in the doorway of a stone house in Germany, sick with the remembrance of a pile of human shit he found in the living room, vomiting sour cherries as an enemy patrol went by. I studied the scars on his leg while I tried to understand the scars on his brain. My war, his war had no relation.

When Bob's troubles started, when the days began to drift, he fought the slow slippage of his mind with vitamins and minerals and exercises for his brain while I tried to nag him back to work. In the late 1970s the children and I begged Bob to stop drinking and go into therapy. We found a kind psychiatrist, and Bob told our housekeeper as he left for his sessions that he was off to the dentist and would be back soon.

"Now, Mr. Crichton, when did this begin?" the doctor asked in his too-calm voice at the first session.

Bob pointed to the War. I was less certain.

But on the way home from that first meeting, Bob put a leaf between his teeth and, cupping his mouth with his hands, began to whistle. "Hey! Mr. Tambourine Man, play a song for me. In the jingle jangle morning I'll come following you . . ."

For a moment, standing in the sun near the Central Park bridle path, with wisteria vines shading the ramble, we thought we had a chance.

CHAPTER 1

We met on an uncommonly soft spring day in March 1951. He was the tallest man I'd ever known—six foot six—and the first man I knew to wear a corduroy suit to work. I was the first girl he had ever known to wear fresh violets in the bosom of a black dress in the morning. I was twenty and he was twenty-six, a war veteran wounded in the Battle of the Bulge. By the end of the afternoon, we were in love.

The day Bob and I met, I may have given an impression of strength I had yet to acquire. At sixteen I had begun to move beyond the gravitational pull of my family. I went to work as a typist and file clerk for *This Week* magazine, a Sunday newspaper supplement, and after work hung out with older pals at the Village Vanguard, drinking milk and smoking reefers with jazz trumpeter Muggsy Spanier. My new best friend, Luci Kaufman, was an orphan, a socialist, a thoughtful young woman who took me to Henry Wallace rallies at Madison Square Garden where I held hands with strangers and sang "This land is my land, this land is your land."

But there were also dreadful bouts of depression. I'd try on new personas like Halloween masks and abandon them as quickly, running back to Luci whose hold on reality was stronger than my own. Along the way I'd come to understand that what I was really running from was not the meanness of my mother or the sad narcissism of my father—in time, I would make peace with them both—but rather their inability to share their interior lives. Their lives seemed orchestrated to meet the demands of form and manner, and if that was achieved, that counted as a life well lived. But those lives could also be the loneliest of lives.

Bob and I met in a corridor at *Argosy* magazine where I'd worked for two years as an assistant articles editor. Bob had joined the staff after I'd left, and in less than a year, had become something of a legend, fired and rehired on a regular basis. His boss—my old boss—had warned me that Bob would never settle down. He drank too much, he wasn't made for marriage. That didn't matter. Meeting Bob in that dim hall, he fell into nominal stranger talk, but only for a sentence or two before shifting out. Using words like a quick-sketch artist, he began to draw the outline of his life, engaging us both in a verbal dance more intimate than either of us intended.

We stepped into his office, a cubicle he shared with an older woman named Margaret who continued copy-editing while we kept talking. I no longer recall the words, only their intensity. I can see Bob in his corduroy suit, arms folded, hand beneath his chin, standing with one foot on a pile of magazines stacked by his desk.

"What are you thinking?" he asked.

But he already knew the answer. I was home.

Bob had gone to Harvard, I had barely finished high school. He loved Eliot and Joyce and had studied *Finnegan's Wake.* I was still quoting Edna St. Vincent Millay and had never heard of Henry Miller. But I had a great dress and very long legs, and we married six weeks later. In fact, it was four months, but we collaborated on the lie. Six weeks is what we told ourselves, the children, anyone who asked. Bob said six weeks seemed closer to the truth.

I learned that he was Catholic when he ordered fish for lunch that Friday. The Vatican still reeked of anti-semitism in 1951. Sex was in the air but there was no way to ask a man on a first date do you believe in contraception. It was a while before I understood that Bob went in and out of religion, influenced as much by his radical father Kyle as his church-going mother May. Some days he was an Irish Catholic like May, other days a Scottish leftist like Kyle, both forces strong and often at war within him.

I had grown up in a tight little island of a world, drilled in the mannerisms that confirmed Our Crowd—German Jews, students of propriety who wore white gloves in public, didn't eat garlic and didn't use their hands when they spoke. Bob never noticed. His life was not encumbered by other people's rules.

It was ten days before I agreed to go to his apartment in Greenwich Village. We met at a bar ankle-deep in sawdust, surrounded by couples far more relaxed than we. When we reached the shabby four-story building on West 12th Street, Bob slapped his pockets for his house key and, failing to find it, tapped on a ground-floor window. I never saw the woman who threw open the window, never learned her name. It all happened so quickly. But as he hoisted himself up over the sill with an assurance born of practice, I could hear a warm exchange of voices and almost ran away. Some moments later Bob opened the front door and pulled me inside.

"Who was the woman in the window, how do you know her?"

"Why does it matter?"

"Were you lovers, are you lovers ...?"

"She's a friend now, don't you worry."

"But who is this woman who opens her window at eleven in the evening?"

"What's the difference? We're inside now."

Bob lived in a one-room apartment at the end of a long dingy hall, lined with doors that went nowhere. There was a small alcove at the room's entrance with a bureau on one side and a stove on the other. I stood in the hall while he began to tidy up, taking the hairbrush off the burner and moving the frying pan off the bureau. When he opened the oven to put the pan away, a mouse ran out behind the couch, and I wanted to go home.

"My God, don't be a sissy!"

"But I'm tired."

"Stay a minute."

"I don't like mice."

"He won't be back, stay a minute, then I'll take you —"

"Who's that woman?"

"What's it matter?"

"Can I go now?"

"If you have to—but first I want to play a record."

His couch ran along a window that looked out onto a courtyard the landlord called a garden. We listened to *Chants d'Auvergne* on a well-used 78 record, when through the night-sounds of the Village, I heard a voice from upstairs calling: "Bob, Bob, Bob." He said it was a cat. I didn't believe him and took a taxi home.

But as I fell asleep that night, I thought of his face as he had put me in the cab, of the flowers in the beer bottle decorating his bathroom, of the books on his table and the sweet sounds of the Auvergne. I knew I would go back to this curious and dangerous man.

He sent a memo from the office about our Intense Adventure while I continued to swing between love and suspicion. I was running from the safe gray men who made my grandmothers so happy, dancing school partners chosen because they were taller than I, those boys with their comfortable expectations and the certain knowledge their lives would progress as their parents' had before them, from a world in which we knew who we were and little ever changed.

I realize now that when I first met Bob, I was both more independent and more needy than I recalled or let on. A snapshot that languished for years in a folder of orphaned photos brings me back to the confusing mixture that I was. In the picture, I was eighteen, maybe nineteen, posing on a windswept bluff in Haiti. The island was little in the news in the late 1940s but Bill O'Brian, a cartoonist friend from work, had sailed to Haiti and spoke of an unusually friendly people, of swimming in a warm and azure-colored sea, of Haitian painters

Americans had yet to hear of. Paradise, he called it, and so I flew to Paradise.

It was not until I found myself standing in line in the crowded arrival shed in Port au Prince, taller and whiter than anyone around, that I realized I had landed in a French-speaking country where virtually everyone was Black and nothing was familiar. I had booked a modest room in a small hotel in the hills above the city. The lobby at the Splendid looked like the set for a movie I had yet to see: desultory ceiling fans, rangy potted plants, a well-washed tiled floor and a clutch of mysterious men in European suits who spoke among themselves, never shed their dark glasses, and arrived and departed in the largest cars on the island.

The manager of the Splendid, a generous and ebullient woman named Madame Frankel, who wore no-shaped dresses and spoke a little English, always seemed relieved to see the men drive off. Madame had a lover, a dark-haired Frenchman smaller than she, but he had strong arms and a scar on his cheek and was said to have escaped from Devil's Island. On occasion they invited me to dinner at their villa where I laughed at jokes in French that I didn't understand. Dominating their living room, otherwise a rather formal salon, was a shiny white refrigerator stocked with Coca-Cola and assorted liquors. For the first time in my life, I drank vermouth cassis and understood the fascination of the unfamiliar: the delight of being a stranger in a strange land.

My second Sunday on Haiti was Easter Sunday and a young Haitian doctor who had been introduced by Madame drove me out into the country to watch a religious procession winding down the mountain: men carrying paintings of a Black Christ and Virgin Mary, banners with voodoo symbols floating in comfortable juxtaposition with the Cross. The music, the drums, the joyous sounds of homemade wooden whistles, the skinny bare-legged boys and dressed-up girls, the banners and flowers, the sweetness in the air, the handsome young doctor, all touched my heart. And moving to a cheaper room, I extended my stay.

In our days together, the Doctor led me beyond the tourist paths into villages in Haiti's interior where he was studying yaws, a leprosy-like disease that quite literally ate people alive and is now readily treatable by anti-biotics. Behind the market in Port au Prince, not far from the elaborate Presidential Palace, the Doctor took me into a shantytown built on a swamp. In the heat and stench of the sewage, only the flies seemed truly alive. Travelers deprived of language, history and a guide like the Doctor can all too easily confuse Paradise and Hell.

In the cool of a late afternoon, the Doctor and I made our way through a field of wild grasses and then hand in hand climbed an idyllic hill as wild parrots commented on our passing. Time ceased and context faded. But then, in one of those coincidences only God can arrange, my grandfather Feiner's law partner appeared like Jehovah, glowering down on us from the crest of the hill. The Doctor and I spoke little on the ride back to the hotel, but it was clear to both of us that I was headed home.

Something about Bob and the way he lived his life connected to those moments on Haiti, the force of being outside the world I knew too well. Bob woke every morning glad to be alive. I woke with a checklist of required obligations. I knew I would live forever. Bob knew he would not.

Nothing in my life had prepared me for Bob. When he celebrated our escape from a tense family dinner by hanging by his knees from a tree at 70th Street and Park Avenue, I was embarrassed by the boisterousness of the gesture—and delighted by his exaggerated ways.

"You're drunk," I said.

"I'm happy," he answered.

The next day he sent me a note:

You're spoiled, but I love you.
I am spoiled and I know you love me.
Together we shall unspoil each other.

When we began to live together, Bob proved to be far more house-trained than I: neater, smarter, better with money. I'd been taught the rules, but he had had the practice. I was born almost rich, he was born almost poor. We would lie in bed and argue over my purchase of ground sirloin and imported French peas. As he tried to teach me to live on $50 a week, he took buses and subways while I hailed taxis.

BAD HABITS OF MISS JUDY FEINER
she always leaves the milk out of the ice box so it
turns warm . . . and then it curdles

and finally it is so sour
it has to be thrown out.

Her adoring fiancé,
    Robert

The notes would come for most of our life together. Letters would arrive at the office door, appear on my desk, be buried under pillows: letters from Bob I now hold in my hand all these years later.

The morning of our wedding, lying in a bath while a short-notice caterer cluttered the kitchen and my mother fussed over flowers, I tried to disconnect two warring emotions. The interesting man, the tall funny handsome experienced man I was about to marry, had composed a poem about my thighs I was too shy to read. I was searching for security but suspected that security was not part of the contract. As I began to dress, I remembered that years before, goaded by another handsome boy, I had flown off a ten-foot diving board only to be dragged half-conscious from the pool.

The night before the wedding, Bob's brother Andy and his wife Elizabeth had tried to bring our two families together, the Feiners and the Crichtons. My father and mother, divorced and scarcely speaking, carried between them twenty-two years of smoldering anger. Bob's father Kyle stuttered and fingered his cigar and wore his porkpie hat for much of the evening. Bob's mother May and his sister Viv, both joylessly polite, informed us during dinner that they could not come to the wedding and hoped we understood. The priest forbade their attendance not because I was Jewish but because Bob and I were being married outside the Church. Kyle grew sad-eyed and Bob retreated while I tried not to cry. When I lost the struggle, Andy walked me around the block.

Dinner proceeded on a wave of endless small talk. My father Ben and Kyle, two large men on opposite sides of the political fault line, circled each other with words, agreeing on little if anything at all. The week that Bob and I had met, Kyle had been cited as a communist by the House UnAmerican Activities Committee. In 1951, the fear of communism was a national obsession but I had yet to understand the consequences to Kyle, or to the country.

My father's politics were predictable, and like his father's before him, committed to preserving the status quo. Throughout the evening, the question "Are you now or have you ever been a member of the Communist Party?" was reflected in my father's eyes. But he would never get a satisfactory answer, nor would the Committee. Kyle would never discuss his political past, never recant, and never name names. And he would remain in professional limbo for the rest of his life.

The evening ended early, with May warning Bob that we had a long day ahead.

Nothing about our wedding day was like other people's weddings. While the guests milled about in the stifling summer heat in my grandmother's apartment on East 79th Street, Bob had yet to appear and my mother conjured dire scenarios I didn't want to hear. I later learned he was at Brooks Brothers, tending to the last of his pre-wedding chores. Earlier that morning, hungover and sleepy, he had raced off to buy wedding attire. Finding a white linen jacket—44 extra long—he handed the salesclerk check number one on the joint bank account we had opened just the day before. The clerk called the bank for validation, but our account had yet to clear. And so the fuss began. In the hallowed halls of Brooks Brothers where men seldom raised their voices, Bob talked the manager into gambling that he was indeed the gentleman he claimed to be.

Carrying the jacket, whistling happily, sweating profusely, he raced back to our apartment where his brother Andy, who had been waiting for him for hours, said, "So you have time to whistle, eh?" and slugged him on the jaw.

The next day *The New York Times* reported that my uncle Richard Rodgers played Mendelssohn's Wedding March as I trailed my giddy sixteen-year-old sister Margot into the living room. The wedding notice did not mention that the piano was out of tune, that Kyle was crying over May's boycott of the wedding, that Bob's jaw was red, or that the judge who married us was an old Tammany Hall hack who lectured us like children about the long road ahead.

The ceremony was short but took forever and then in the girlhood room I never liked, I changed into my going-away dress, and Bob and I fled.

Standing on the corner of Third Avenue beneath the El tracks on the hottest day of that summer, Bob told me that before we left for our honeymoon in Havana, we had to clean out the 12th Street apartment or forfeit a month's rent. Bob wanted to take the El down to the Village. He thought it would be romantic. I made the case for a taxi. I scrubbed the toilet in my going-away dress, he streaked his new jacket cleaning the oven. Little about the day went the way I thought it should. For the first but not the last time, I found myself wondering if I should have married one of the good gray predictable men my grandmothers favored. And then the apartment was clean and I was delighted I had not.

All I could see on that hot night in Havana, with the prancing bellhop fussing with the windows, was the big bed, the double bed that all but filled our room. Bob flopped on the bed in his worn loafers and went to sleep while I tipped the bellhop far too much or far too little. I thought that Bob was teasing and would turn into a proper husband but he would not respond. I spent the next few hours in the lobby, watching rich tourists leave for the casino while I practiced smoking with the new gold cigarette-holder Bob had bought me at Dunhill's the week before. In a mahogany case by the concierge's desk was our wedding photo and the wedding announcement from *The New York Times*.

In the morning Bob struggled to the window in the bright glare of the view overlooking Havana. He was as disoriented as I was.

"You're a nice girl to take away for a weekend," he said, "But for the rest of my life?"

Panic filled the room, filled the light, filled the bed. He was trying to be funny but it didn't work at all.

As we went down to breakfast in silence, I began to plan for a quiet divorce. But several hours later, floating in an oversized pool, another set of fantasies took over. I swam underwater till I reached where Bob was treading water by the pool's edge, put my arms around his waist and pressed my breasts against his back. As he rose up out of the water and slowly turned to face me, I realized to my horror it wasn't Bob at all.

"Oh, I thought you were my husband," I said to the stranger who was short and fat and hairy and did not believe a word I said.

Bob laughed as he handed me a towel and led me away from the confusion of the pool. For years, he would tease me about my other lover who winked and blinked and leered at me for the rest of our stay in Havana.

CHAPTER 2

B ob knew—he had always known—that he was a writer. He told my father he would quit his job and settle down to work on a book. "What will you live on?" my father had asked. "Your daughter," Bob answered. It was the logical solution.

We had rented a two-room apartment in a small building on a quiet sunny corner at 30th Street and Lexington Avenue. The large bright room with an ornate marble fireplace became our home. The second room became the junk room for the laundry we could not seem to get to, the wedding presents we didn't use or want, the unpaid bills we couldn't face. I had never learned to iron or clean house, and let the dustballs gather and the food turn moldy. But I had a job and Bob settled in to work on the book he had started at Harvard.

That fall I wrote Bob this letter:

All my life I've known that my ambition—my flairs
—could never build anything very important on
their own. But although I lack the craftsmanship,

the basic intelligence, the education I have things to say. I want the things to be said—and I have always known and wanted and always prayed that someday I could in some way contribute and help someone with the ability to say them. If you can spend the rest of your life writing, nothing could more directly fulfill all I have always wanted.

Bob had been startled to discover how ill-educated I was. I was startled, too. I had no real schooling after sixth grade. Depending on my family's fortunes and my mother's curious notions, I wandered from one institution to another, writing poetry, failing math, and learning to slide by. I managed to graduate at sixteen from The Knox School for Girls, a third-rate boarding school in upstate New York.

But books had always been at the center of Bob's life. In high school, he wrote a twenty-page essay on "The Literature of the World," which his teacher suggested was not a report but a program for a life study. Bob's literary template for the educated man began with Chaucer and galloped through the English canon and the French. Sixteen pages later, he declared: "I am now with my back against the wall. I have three pages left and have not covered Russian literature." To leave out the Russians, he wrote, was "like missing the white elephant at the circus."

Dead Souls was a "hilariously funny story," Turgenev's hero was an "upstart nihilist." Tolstoy was "the most natural of all the world's writers," and so I was started on Tolstoy. Bob had promised to marry me if I lost twenty pounds and read *War and Peace,* and I did both.

Almost every night, before we went to sleep, Bob read aloud, tracking our progress in his diary, along with descriptions of making love:

Wed.
By the time dinner is over it is late. I wanted to
read *Don Juan in Hell* but no book so we read
Glaspell's incredibly apt *A Jury of Her Peers*, and
an excellent story of loneliness and an analysis by
Wallace Stegner called "The Traveler." Und zie to
schloffin.

Thurs.
We read Shaw's *Man and Superman* and it brings
a resolve to get more intellectual and less social
stimulation in our lives. Then to bed and sweet
sleep which is one other purpose for which beds
were invented.

The book Bob was quitting his other work to focus on was called *The Minnow Fishers,* a portrait of his Catholic boyhood which he had started writing in college. Was it a memoir or a novel? I suspect a bit of both. When Bob was five or six, his family had moved from Albuquerque to an Irish neighborhood—what his brother Andy called "gray collar"—in Jackson Heights, Queens. It was this world the book tried to capture, where immigrants' sons became cops, and cops' sons competed to become King O' the Hill in the empty lots. Bob played stickball, ran with the Irish Dukes, and wrestled with the mysteries of the Church during Mass on Sundays.

> When someone was seriously sick the priest was
> called to administer the last rites with fresh white
> linens and beeswax candles and the oils and ashes
> and the Sacred Host right in the house. The rite is
> called Extreme Unction and I lived in terror that it
> would some day occur in my house.

> The phrase long before had become one word,
> Extramunction, and across the elevated tracks
> where the less successful lived, the families who
> had never recovered from the Famine or were just
> off the boat, shortened it even more, to
> Stramunction.

The news always traveled through the neighborhood the same way.

— I suppose you heard what happened to
Hanrahan's father.

— Father Reilly was called to the house.
Stramunction.

So, there it was then. Out in the open. Without
needing the words. The death sentence. Hanrahan
was as good as in the box.

Bob wrote about the Blessed Sacrament Elementary School and Sister Theresa who had the eyes of a cop and prepared Bob and his classmates for their First Communion. Bob modeled Blessed Sacrament after his own parochial school in Jackson Heights, St. Joan of Arc, founded by the Grey Nuns whose mission was "to proclaim the Gospel of Jesus to all, especially the poor and the needy." Bob took issue with their methods.

"Now don't bite it, whatever you're about," she
had told us. "It's the Body and Blood of Christ in
your mouth. Let Father Meehan put it on your
tongue and then let it melt away. I've told all of
you what happened to Timmy Monahan and you
don't want it happening to you."

I stared down the rows of other boys, all dressed like myself, black in our First Communion suits, remembering the words of Sister Theresa. Poor Timmy Monahan walking back from the altar, his mouth gushing blood after biting into the Sacred Host. I could see him lying in the aisle, his mouth running blood out onto the dull red marble floor, while Father Meehan washed his head in the holy oil giving him the last rites.

In the book, Bob's friend Emmet McDonell, the youngest member of the Irish Dukes, is determined to put the Timmy Monahan story to the test. Emmet is too young to take Communion, so Bob would accept the Sacred Host, slip it into his pocket and sneak it to Emmet who would then take it home and pierce it with the prongs of a fork. That would put the lie to the mystery forever. But when Bob and his classmates line up in church in their new Communion suits, Sister Theresa's presence hovers over them "like the heavy black mantle which covered her head." At the altar rail, Bob accepts the Host and then, just as Sister Theresa had instructed, lets it melt away. "Why didn't Emmet ever want to believe anything," he wonders.

On a St. Patrick's Day outing, out of sight of the nuns, out of sight of any parent, Bob and the Dukes head out to

Staten Island with Emmet and Emmet's older brother Micky. It is while they are roasting potatoes on a junk-littered hill that Emmet disappears. But Emmet was always disappearing. Earlier in the day, down at the Battery waiting for the ferry, he had wandered off to find his friend, the goiter man. Now in ones and twos, the boys set out to find him. Bob can hear Micky somewhere down the road calling for his brother.

Across the river in Manhattan, the lights are coming on when Kevin Riordan silently waves Bob back to the crest of the hill. From there he can see Emmet's body floating face up in the old rock quarry with "his mackinaw billowing up around him like he was lying in a feather bed." Kevin and Bob stand for a moment facing the wind, trying to stop crying, and then without a word to any of the others, set off for the long trip back to Queens.

"Did that really happen?" I asked Bob. "Is the story fact or fiction?"

"If you feel it's the truth," Bob said, "Well, that's what it is."

As Bob settled down to write *The Minnow Fishers*, I fought the distance between us. I couldn't accept his quiet withdrawal. "I'm here," he would say, "Isn't that enough?"

I wasn't certain. He kept letters from old girlfriends: Marian who wore a leather dress from Paris that had shrunk in the rain, and Freddie, the brilliant Freddie, one of the first woman graduates of Harvard Law School. When Bob wasn't home, I read and reread their letters searching for insights I couldn't define. Do you really think I'd leave you? The question went unanswered but I was far more fearful than he understood.

Bob and I were children of Freud: amateur analysts who lay in bed at night struggling to explain ourselves to ourselves and to each other while reveling in our differences. The Crichtons were so poor, they had Jell-O on their birthdays. My mother's parents, Stella and Percy Lansburgh, had thirteen servants. Thirteen servants? There were thirteen servants. Well, maybe eleven. The upstairs maid and the downstairs maid, the cook and her assistant . . .

Until I was nine, when my stockbroker grandfather Percy Lansburgh went bankrupt, had a heart attack and died, we spent our summers in a large white stucco house in Scarsdale he had built in 1904. Inside, the house was dark and heavy, the shades kept drawn against the sun. Beyond the house and the formal rose garden, the potting sheds and hothouse, was a well-appointed two-story doll house large enough for me to crawl into until one summer, following a long winter's growth spurt, my shoulders became wedged on the second-floor landing while the rest of me stretched down the staircase. My grandmother was beside herself, fearing the gardener would do damage trying to free me. The fire department was called—my grandmother said they were more experienced with extractions—and from that moment on, the dollhouse was off-bounds. But in front of the main house, at the edge of the great lawn, stood a giant weeping willow with branches that swept the ground. The shade of that weepimg willow became my hide-away— from the sun and from Fraulein, my hated German nurse.

Fraulein dominated my life, and I loathed her. After breakfast every morning when my cereal was finished, when I had folded my napkin, I would request permission to visit my grandparents in their bedroom. They took breakfast in pale green single beds on elaborate trays with embroidered doilies, napkins and crystal bud vases. My grandfather wore long pajama tops made by Aunt Mary, his old wet nurse who wore long dark dresses and lived in the attic with her sewing machine. While my grandfather studied the newspaper and my grandmother worked on her menus, I lingered in their bedroom redolent with perfume, filled with roses and satin covers, sharing toast thin as wafers until Fraulein retrieved me, dragging me to a bathroom at the foot of the stairs.

"I can't," I'd whimper.

That never deterred her.

"I don't have to!" I shouted.

I was handed a book and placed on the toilet. Summers were hot, the seat stuck to my skin. Sometimes Fraulein would wind up the Victrola in a nearby sitting room and listen to arias while I tested my sphincter muscles. Always she hovered just beyond the door. Whatever I accomplished was subject to inspection. Sometimes the parlor maid was brought in for confirmation, or my Aunt Jane on her way to tennis, rarely my mother who usually stayed in bed. It was Fraulein who passed judgment, who declared when I passed muster, Fraulein who declared when the toilet could be flushed.

I have no memory of Fraulein leaving or understanding of why she was dismissed. But I remember Nini, how she arrived and how she left. On the day Nini first came to our apartment in New York City, she took me into the kitchen and made us both Swiss chocolate sandwiches with butter on rye bread. On rainy afternoons, she set a tea at the nursery table and taught me songs in French that I remember to this day. On Christmas when my mother and father went off to a party, and I began to cry, Nini took me into her room and told me that she was lonely, too. I had just turned five, she may have been forty. That we loved each other was beyond dispute.

A half year later on a late spring afternoon, I was called into the living room. At the suggestion of my mother, I sat on a yellow brocade chair. My mother and Nini faced me from the couch, Nini blinking in a way I had never seen before. "I have something to tell you," my mother began. "Nini is leaving—"

I began to scream and before either woman could move, I threw up all over the chair, the oriental rug and my brand new hand-smocked dress. "She can't go!" I screamed.

But Nini said "I love you" and as my mother tried to intervene, I threw up once more and Nini was gone.

That evening, my mother told me she was about to have another baby, that we needed a trained nurse able to handle us both. For years I searched for Nini on the street and in the park. Every bus held the promise of seeing her again. I begged my mother to invite her for a visit but my mother knew better.

I told Bob about Nini but with Bob, memory tended to work backwards. Childhood stories would have to wait. Six years after the War, the War was seldom from his mind.

Bob in his army jacket with the Railsplitters insignia

CHAPTER 3

———————————

The first time Bob exploded, we had no explanation. We were sitting at the counter of a Village coffee shop one evening when a bunch of rowdy kids began horsing around. Twirling on their stools, the kids start spritzing each other and accidentally spritzed Bob. Without any warning, Bob leapt off his stool, collared a kid easily a foot shorter than he was, and shook the boy until I feared Bob would break his neck. Someone called the cops, others grabbed Bob's arm, and I was embarrassed, which was not the right reaction. I paid the check and somehow got Bob out of the coffee shop and into a taxi.

At home we undressed in silence and began a conversation that never ended.

Nothing in my life had prepared me for the violence raging in Bob's head. For me, the War was still an abstract. We had grown up in a world steeped in 19th century values. World War I had ended only six years before Bob was born. Every Armistice Day throughout his childhood and mine, old veterans with their medals and division caps sold red paper poppies to raise money for the wounded. On the mornings of November 11th, the 11th hour of the 11th day of the 11th month, no matter where we were, we bowed our collective heads in silence to commemorate the dead and mark the moment when the war had officially ended. Every parade in the 1930s ended with a cadre of the last living veterans of the Civil War, fragile old men wrapped in lap robes with small American flags taped to the arms of their wheelchairs. Every generation had its war. By their very natures, men were expected to be brave, to keep their own counsel about the horrors of war. No one talked about the psychic cost of combat.

For Bob, the war was always with him but his stories emerged in disconnected fragments. Some would be repeated over and over: the November day in the beet field in Belgium when he killed four young German soldiers.

As a boy Bob had learned the A. E. Houseman poem, "The Day of Battle":

> But since the man that runs away Lives to
> die another day,
> And cowards' funerals, when they come
> Are not wept so well at home.

Therefore, though the best is bad,
Stand and do the best my lad;
Stand and fight and see your slain,
And take the bullet in your brain.

Early in November 1951, Bob abandoned work on *The Minnow Fishers*, and began making notes for a book about the war, *The Poor Miserable Stinking Rotten Infantry*. Paraphrasing Goethe, he said, "One should write the book that only he can write."

Bob would work on the War Book on and off for the rest of his life. There were many beginnings, many titles: *Memoirs of a Bad Soldier* was the last. But for thirty years the underlying ideas remained the same: "There is absolutely no value we hold essential to life which war does not twist and bend into ludicrous patterns."

The basic facts of Bob's experiences in the War were not very complicated. Bob was nineteen, just out of high school, a private in a rifle company, Company L, in the 84th Infantry Division, and at six foot six too tall for the service. But he was young and strong and the army was no longer measuring men too closely. During basic training, he searched for clothes to fit him and rarely succeeded. He went into battle wearing a formal overcoat and undersized boots that all but destroyed his feet.

In our bed on 36th Street, his toes were still white and gnarled, lifeless yet inordinately sensitive. The only time I ever saw him acknowledge pain was when someone inadvertently stepped on his foot. Most of the men in the unit were as young as he, eighteen or nineteen: country boys from Tennessee with little to no schooling who could put a rifle or carbine together faster than Bob could read the instructions.

Bob landed in France on November 2nd, 1944, convinced that by training and circumstance he had been preconditioned for war.

Born on the battlefields of the Irish neighborhood
I had grown up in, where we dug real trenches and
strung real barbed wire and shot at each other with
BB shot until Jackie Mulligan had his eye shot out.
After that it was rocks for bullets and much larger
rocks for hand grenades and always the frightening but exhilarating need to stand fast and stick it
out when the others, the enemy, came attacking
across the lot with their bags of rocks.

Sometimes men on their way home from work
stopped to watch our war but no one ever tried to
stop it. Some of the men had been In It and they
gave us tips on how to build dugouts.

Then my father began making money and we
moved away into middle class respectability and
my war was over. Romantic notions die hard,
however, and so does language steeped and
soaked in legend and reverence and mystery.

In Flanders fields the poppies blow
Between the crosses, row on row . . .

They were raced to the front by truck, and thrown into
an attack on the Siegfried Line. The Allies had been
advancing all autumn, pursuing the Germans through
much of Belgium and France. But now the advance was
stalled. Along the front from the Dutch border and south
to the Rhine, the Allies met unparalleled resistance. By
mid-December they would be outnumbered by the
Germans three to one—in some areas, ten to one.

Bob had headed off to war eager to discover how he
would measure up. He didn't much like what he found. In
the small ancient city of Geilenkirchen, on the western
border of Germany, the 94th fought street by street and
house by house in a cold, incessant rain. The roads
leading into the town were knee deep in mud, slowing
down supply trains. Casualties were high. 1944 was one
of the coldest winters in European history. By the end of
November the rain turned to sleet, then snow, then

blinding blizzards. The temperature at night hung below zero. The men were always cold, always hungry, and suffered from frostbite, pneumonia and exhaustion. Trapped in a foxhole under heavy mortar fire, nothing from basic training seemed to apply. Bob wrote about the moment "when the balance between performing one's duty and staying alive begins to tilt toward survival, when the good soldier tends to degenerate into the bad." He walked through corpses on a snow-covered hill, rejoicing in his own survival, guilty for rejoicing.

For weeks Bob never changed his clothes. The skin on his back would bear the scars of layered filth forever. Well-insulated footwear with rubber soles had been sent to Europe but hadn't managed to reach the front lines. The ill-fitting leather boots worn by infantrymen would become an acknowledged scandal, but not in time. The troops were ordered to change their socks and massage their feet every day to avoid trench foot. It was cynical advice. Bob yearned for fresh socks, prayed for fresh socks. He had written home begging his parents for socks. If gangrene set in, if the skin went from white to black, a man could lose his toes, then his feet, and if the infection was not halted in time he would lose his life. Fifty years later, historian Stephen Ambrose wrote in *Citizen Soldiers*, "trench foot put more men out of action than German 88s, mortars or machine-gun fire. During the winter of 1944-45, some forty-five thousand men had to be pulled out of the front line because of trench foot—the equivalent of three full infantry divisions."

For weeks, weather kept the Allied reconnaissance planes grounded. The strategists were blind, unaware of the buildup of German forces in the east. On December 16th, the Germans went on the offensive, breaking through the American line. Throughout the Battle of the Bulge, four divisions, including the 84th, were surrounded, trapped in the Ardennes forest. By Christmas, supplies were running low. The Germans were so close that Bob could hear them talking at night. Every man in his platoon, apart from Bob, was now a replacement. His commanding officer, two platoon leaders and the majority of Company L were gone—dead or wounded. He was fighting alongside men whose names he never knew and didn't want to learn. And the worst was yet ahead.

On January 3rd, in blinding snow, the American counter-offensive began. When the order came, Bob's platoon was holed up in a huge barn. For the briefest moment he conjured up a summer spent in Vermont, could smell the clover in the hay, remembered the dry cool calm near the ice pit where it was always cool. He was a boy again, and safe. Then came the orders. The 84th was moving into what Ambrose would describe in *Citizen Soldier* as "one of the most God awful offensives of this or any other war." It took four brutal weeks for the Allies to beat their way back to the German border, to retake the ground they had lost. 77,000 Americans were killed or wounded.

On January 26th, ten miles south of Malmedy, the 84th Division began hammering the town of St. Vith. A mortar round exploded behind Bob, and a piece of shrapnel dug into his shoulder. He was taken off line and declared unfit for further duty. After two months of continuous battle, he was in danger of losing his feet to frostbite and gangrene, as well as his mind. He was shipped off to England where he spent four months in an army hospital.

Among his notes for the War Book that I found many years later:

> . . . loss of innocence, yes, but also the journey
> to less of a man, to the state of shooting rabbits
> with bazookas, shooting pianos, shooting
> pictures, bibles, bombing fish. See the fish in
> the pool throw a hand grenade in, to this depth
> I had come, to this brand of personal miserable
> madness. Should I begin with shooting the
> piano, the skewering of four Germans for no
> real purpose at all, the lazy laconic way of it,
> the aimless almost thoughtless way of it . . .

It was clear that the psychic gyroscope which had kept Bob in balance before the war had been knocked awry.

For Bob, stories were always where the truth was concealed and revealed, usually at the same time. A friend said Bob was the kind of person who went around the corner to buy a cigar and when he came back, it was the Odyssey. Grand stories, tall stories, stories spun from the lint of everyday life. I'd watch Bob take the most modest of elements, shape and refine them until he'd created something he considered worth the telling. He'd go out for a pack of cigarettes and return two hours later after breaking up a brawl at the candy store, helping a bartender in a storm batten down an awning, finding and returning lost wallets, lost children, lost dogs.

Sometimes his stories were inventions to cover time lost in a bar or time with a woman, I would have to suspect. But some of the more preposterous stories turned out to be true. Long into our marriage, Bob returned late from a walk before breakfast in Yorkshire, England having found a lost lamb. "A lost lamb, for God's sake?" Yes, a lost baby lamb trapped on a rock in a swollen brook that needed to be rescued and returned to its mother. I didn't believe him but as we checked out of our inn later that morning, the innkeeper knocked ten pounds off our bill in gratitude for Bob's rescue of the lamb.

With Bob, the line between fantasy and reality was often exceedingly fine. What might have made the War Book so hard to write was his need to be faithful to the real experience when his whole being was inclined toward embellishment. Bob had reached an impasse on the War Book, torn between revealing the truth as he knew it, and the sense that he was violating the veteran's code of silence. He was mowing down old myths that had provided comfort for generations. Bob was writing about men pushed too far, men transformed into zombies and dismissed as malingerers. In time, statistics on neuro-psychiatric breakdowns in Europe would be published that confirmed his thesis. But in 1952, Bob was odd man out. He didn't see the War as others saw it.

> War was survival not of the fittest but of the most careful. Men fought not out of patriotism but because they had no choice, it was the only way home.

> There was always a Western urge to believe in the efficacy of experience, good or bad, that out of exposure to harsh experience, the survivors are

rewarded with some kind of special security or immunity. It is presumed that the veterans of experience are becoming wiser and stronger, more tenacious, more capable, more courageous and even more human.

There is magic involved in all this, which soldiers themselves want to believe in and tend to perpetuate, that the wisdom of experience, so hard learned and hard earned, makes one magically immune to rifle fire and artillery shells. Green troops drop like blue-tailed flies in the long walk across the open field but the shrapnel doesn't search out the grizzled sergeant. Or how else would he get grizzled?

There must be some virtue and some reward to all this surviving.

But it didn't work that way. There was no immunity in combat. Each moment in combat lessened your chances of surviving the next. Grizzled sergeants *did* die, and experience only made a man more apprehensive, not less. Other armies rotated their front line units, but Americans kept infantrymen on line until they were wounded or killed or their nervous systems were destroyed. It was a brutal and inefficient system. There were far more breakdowns than anyone acknowledged at the time, and historians and journalists were still supporting the myth of the *battle-hardened veterans.*

Bob went back to work on *The Minnow Fishers* but never really put the War Book aside, and the nightmares continued. Again and again he conjured the night when on the outskirts of Geilenkirchen, he had hidden in a farmhouse, retching from sour cherries he had found in the basement and devoured, and the noxious presence of human shit in the living room. As he stifled his own nausea and remained silent, he let a German patrol pass by unchallenged, a moment that he considered cowardice and haunted him throughout his life. He was reliving the war with almost monotonous regularity. Trying to soothe him, I would call him brave, which irritated him to despair.

Nothing with Bob was ever black or white. One evening he ran into an army buddy in the Pennsylvania Hotel bar and brought him home for dinner. Over tuna casserole, his platoon mate relived the moment when he lay bleeding and screaming in an open field in Belgium and Bob crawled out under heavy fire to drag him back to safety. But it wasn't only the buddy Bob was brave enough to save. Bob's friend had gone into combat carrying a photo album with pictures of his wife. He'd carried the album all through basic training, across the

Atlantic and into battle, and he'd had the album with him when he was shot. After he was safely in the hands of the medics, he began to weep not from the pain, he said, but because he'd dropped the photo album in the field. Bob headed out and brought the photo album back.

In our early years together, we often went to Pavia, a tiny French restaurant across the street from our apartment, with a dozen or so small candlelit tables, a limited menu and a lot of charm. Five dollars covered two entrees, a glass of wine for Bob, two coffees, and the right to linger as long as we wished. The waiter didn't hover, the busboy brought us extra bread, and Bob exercised his French that was more attitude and charm than proficiency, and talked about his days in Paris.

After the War, after months in an English hospital recovering from frostbite and shrapnel wounds, Bob re-enlisted to spend six months in Paris and was placed in charge of an ice cream plant on the edge of the city, a curious and pleasant duty.

Bob in Paris after the War

A photo from his time there shows Bob in a silk aviator's scarf tucked into his army jacket, pomaded hair brushed into a pompadour high on his forehead. He looked more like a bit player in a French film than an American GI. He was in disguise, a state of suspended animation, trying to unwind before heading home. At the ice cream plant, he was ordered to stand at the kitchen door at the end of every shift to discourage French employees from making off with army provisions. As the women moved to exit, he could see the packets bulging through their summer dresses. But they would stare him down and make him blush. On a wave of *bon soirs*, they left the plant unchallenged with their priceless parcels of sugar. For this lapse Bob felt no remorse.

That night in Pavia, the owner came over and Bob talked about the jazz clubs and strip joints he'd found on the Left Bank. But the tourist talk didn't last long. It never lasted long. Bob eased into his subject by describing his arrival in France when the leaves were shedding. It was an odd business, he said, there was something humbling and disconcerting about the coming of fall, as if this enormous war weren't bigger than nature. The owner of Pavia signaled to the waiter to bring over a bottle of cognac.

With a well-filled snifter in hand, and the restaurant owner stepping away, Bob took off on the inadequacies of the word *shell*. *Shell* was too thin, too immaterial, for what what it truly was. *"Bomb, hand grenade, tank assault, dive bombing—*those words have weight. *Cannonball* has the deadening power of lead. *Shrapnel—*shrapnel from the shell is the scythe of Mister Death, zum

zum zumming across the field to cut you down to size and collect you for his harvest. Did you know they buried the dead in brown paper bread sacks, in brown paper sacks. . .?"

It was time to go home. The busboy mopping the floor paused to unlock the restaurant's door, and the owner watched, lost in his own thoughts, as we crossed the street to our apartment house.

CHAPTER 4

———————

Place had never been important in my life. There had never been a home where I really felt at home. But the central core in Bob's life was home, and home was still the family farm in Newtown. A few years before the end of the War, May and Kyle had bought an eighteenth-century farmhouse with forty rolling acres of abandoned pasture in southern Connecticut. On the rise above the house was an aging barn and the remnants of Bob's chicken coop. By the time I arrived, the hens were long gone. Bob described the morning when he went out to collect eggs after a powerful windstorm and instead found chicken carnage. His friend Stuart Bartle said the birds died of neglect. Bob's father Kyle said never check an interesting fact, and went back to his crossword puzzle.

Bob knew and loved every foot of the place. He loved the smell of the farm, the textures of the barns and stone walls, the soft grass that surrounded the house, the rough meadow beyond. He knew the trees by their bark and the birds by their songs. Six weeks after we returned to New York from our honeymoon, May finally gave in and invited us to Newtown for the weekend. Bob was profoundly relieved. I found the invitation grudging. Bob didn't care, he needed to go home.

Kyle was warm and welcoming, and I loved him from the start. At fifty-five, he could still hit a baseball about as far as his sons. Kyle had battled tuberculosis since his college years and with only one good lung, he could not make it to first base and always used a runner. On the surface, Kyle was a noisy, witty, gregarious man, but there was a sadness over Kyle that fall. A subpoena from the House Committee on Un-American Activities hung over the household like an ever-present shadow. Once one of the most successful magazine editors and writers in the country, Kyle had been denounced as an Un-American. No magazine would touch him. He was writing books for hire and dipping into his savings. But Scotsmen don't indulge in intimacy easily. The details of Kyle's life —his politics and passions—would be revealed slowly and over time.

May was small and pretty and much the tougher of the pair. That she found me wanting was painfully clear. That Bob was afraid of her made matters worse. But he took me up to the woods to look for lady slippers and to the meadow above the house where the berry patches grew, and we began to plan our life. It was Newtown where we spent our first Christmas together.

Bob and Judy in Newtown, with Andy's son Marc

On December 23rd in a snow so light, it almost looked like fog, we arrived for a Crichton Christmas. Bob's two aunts from St. Louis (one bright, the other vague but cheery), his sister Viv, her husband Clayton and their children, his brother Andy and his wife Elizabeth with three-year-old Marc, their dog, and several friends were all crammed into the small Colonial house. On the porch lay a heap of wet galoshes, one unrecognizable from the next. Fifteen at the table for every meal. Folding cots at night in by-the-way corners. Curfew at ten-thirty. I felt I had passed into the land of Norman Rockwell.

The house on Echo Valley Road,
Newtown, Connecticut

Bob and Andy spent their days jostling and jousting and elbowing each other beneath a basketball hoop tacked to the barn or on the ice pond across the road from the house, sliding on the ice on cardboard boxes. This was not a family to invest in skates. Cardboard boxes were more the Crichton style.

Around five o'clock every afternoon, Kyle would put down his crossword, and May would leave her apron in the kitchen. It was cocktail time in Newtown. There were a score of phrases used to call the assembly together: the sun was over the yardarm, "It's time, boys, time!" Half-gallon bottles of bourbon, gin and vodka, tops loosened for quick refills, stood on the kitchen counter with slices of oranges and maraschino cherries the children loved to filch, along with small green olives for Bob's martinis. Conversations were family competitions and grew more heated with every round of drink.

That first Christmas together, Bob wrote in his diary,

Dec. 23rd
The party where everyone drinks and gradually the children are shunted ignominiously into the background. I drink much too much and then . . . I spill out my fears of alcoholism and in a perverted sort of way both my love and fear of losing Judy and myself. In the morning I am so ashamed I have difficulty facing anyone.

Dec. 24th
We play basketball. Strange old antagonisms appear so much mellowed and tempered by age. Andy still wants to beat me and still freezes up trying. The drinks and the reading of *The Night Before Christmas*. The carols where Liz and Judy and I try to sing correctly with the kids. Dad's ridiculous arrogance and Clayton's mimicry until no one sings again. Judy and I are caught smooching. I cease drinking. "Are you mad at me" "No only a little disappointed."

I can still see Newtown so clearly: the Styrofoam reindeers in the bay window, the Christmas balls atop the gold and crystal candelabra, Bob slounging on the couch, his legs stretching half across the room. I can hear his brother-in-law Clayton's sarcasm and recall my anger and see clearly that moment when we were caught with our hands where our hands were not supposed to be. But I have no recollection—none—that Bob was so fearful about his own drinking so early on.

Drinking was a Crichton tradition and in 1951, when the bickering got out of hand, we made excuses. Writers drank, the Scotch drank, the Irish drank, Bob drank because of his war dreams, because he had been fighting with Kyle or with Andy, because his mother was too tough, because I was too demanding. He would quit when he wanted to quit, of that I had no fear.

My heart is lightened by a note he wrote in his diary on Christmas Day: "Julia tells me Mother is fond of Judy and I begin to be most hopeful for my marriage and my life."

I loved becoming part of this large and rough-and-tumble family who, despite all their tensions, put loyalty to kin above God or the flag. Kyle was the youngest of eleven children in a mythic clan of miners. Two were said to have died of malnutrition before he was born. Posing for a photograph in the early 1900s on the porch of their cabin in western Pennsylvania, the Crichtons declared their ambitions by their posture and their dress. Kyle's brother Harry, wearing jacket, shirt and tie, did not look like the young man who once helped keep the family fed by shooting squirrels and rabbits.

Harry, Kyle, the indomitable Sarah and William Crichton
in western Pennsylvania

In the background, pipe in hand, sits the central character in the family legend: William, Kyle's father, a small, wiry man who could still best his sons at the broad jump when he was over seventy (or so it was said). He had shipped out of Glasgow at the age of sixteen hoping to escape a life in the mines. He had worked as a trapper boy from the time he was ten, and that had been enough.

In 1870, William was shipwrecked off the coast of California, only one of two survivors. He made his way east to the mines of western Pennsylvania and West Virginia. But, as Bob later wrote, he had no intention of staying a miner. William was a determined man. For some twenty years or more, he labored in the mines, eventually working alongside his older sons. Together they pooled every penny not essential for survival and some time before World War I, bought the mine they worked in, fired the boss they hated and became capitalists overnight.

It was a remarkable story of family love and loyalty that embraced the entire clan. The two youngest sons, Kyle and Harry, were sent to Lehigh, "the Harvard of the Alleghenies," as Bob had it. Kyle had been a student of unlimited promise, a college athlete who read Lucretius and then went out and threw the longest forward pass in Lehigh history. Then Kyle began losing weight, coughing up blood, teetering on the edge of nothingness: tuberculosis, the disease for which there was little hope and no cure. His family pulled together the money to send him to St. Joseph's Sanatorium in Albuquerque, New Mexico. There Kyle lay in bed and read, and became a writer instead of a miner, a leftist instead of the

Republican businessmen his brothers would become back in Pennsylvania.

At St. Joseph's, every week or so Kyle lost another friend. Kyle managed to survive as those around him slipped away, but he was not the strong young man he once had been. In a snapshot taken at St. Joseph's, Kyle sits at the bedside of his friend Charlie May who is taking the air wearing a robe made of Indian blankets. Charlie would die a few weeks later. On the back of the photo, Kyle wrote, "Charlie May, the best of men who had no enemies even among those who knew him best."

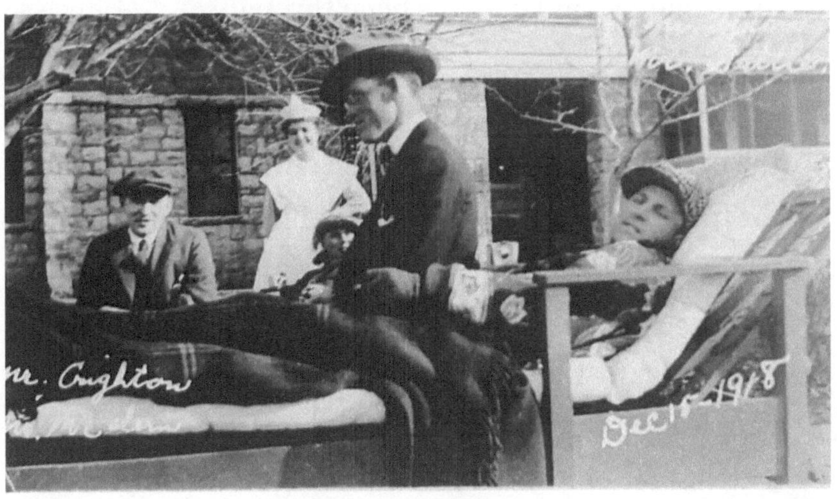

A gaunt Kyle sitting at his friend's bedside; Kyle was 22 years old

Reading Kyle's 1919 diary, the trajectory from Kyle to Bob is clear: the same love of books, sports, politics and women, and the same burdensome understanding of the capriciousness of death, the guilt of the survivor. When Bob came back from the War, it was Kyle who recognized the fear in his son's eyes. We never heard Kyle talk about his days in the sanatorium but after reading a book about Bob's outfit, he wrote Bob this letter:

> You must forgive an old man for his emotions
> because there was little in the book to bring them
> about. It was simply that I felt you there through it
> all. I have kept wanting to write you to say that I
> would feel it a great lack in myself if I ever failed to
> appreciate what you have been through . . .

> I think of myself as a young man and know that
> the experience would have been almost unbearable
> for me. Even through the worst of my t.b. days
> when my friends were dying all around me and my
> chances were as near hopeless as they will ever be,
> I never really thought it was going to get me.
> People are reluctant to talk about death and I had
> a great fear of it when I was your age. It is only
> now that I am getting reconciled to the thought of
> death. . .

> In short I think I understand something of what
> you went through and because of it never intend to

take it lightly. You will probably take this as the
desire of the elderly to get in on the game but it
isn't that. I never wanted you to be a hero and I'm
glad enough that you got back safe; I don't think
I'd have made it.

For years the barometer of Kyle's emotional nature
was set by color in his sputum or a change in his blood
count. The onset of fatigue was so debilitating, it left him
too weak to read or write. I suspect it was May who willed
him back to health. They met at St. Joseph's where she
was a volunteer—and eight years older than he, although
he never knew it. May was Roman Catholic and the
daughter of a Confederate veteran who had moved to
New Mexico before it became a state to serve as a federal
judge for the Indian Territories. May's mother was once
listed among the "Georgia peaches"—antebellum
southern belles—and never accepted all that she and her
family had lost with the Confederacy's defeat. May rarely
mentioned her embittered parents to Bob or his siblings.

Kyle and May married in 1921 and moved into a small
adobe house not far from the sanitorium. Kyle pieced out
a not-quite-living writing advertisements and the occa-
sional article, and handling publicity for John Philip
Sousa and local bookings of lesser lights. Poverty was a
shadow never far away, and Kyle could not forgive

himself for failing to be the provider a man was meant to be.

In the summer of 1922, after Vivienne, his first child, was born, Kyle wrote his father, "I'm a wreck and I fear I'll never be anything else. I'm discouraged, Pap, though I know it isn't manly to be like that. If I had energy and stamina, it would be different. I'm ready to quit. If it hadn't been for you, dear wonderful mother and father, I couldn't have gone this long. I can't tell you how much I love you both."

May refused to succumb to the uncertainties of life. She continued having babies. Andy was born when Viv was just over a year, Bob followed in 1925. Three children in three years: Bob always said the doctor delivered the three as part of "a three-baby deal." The small adobe house, with a patch of dry dust that served as a yard, was filled with babies.

The force in May's life, however, was not the children, never the children, but the extraordinary man she had met on the porch at St. Joseph's, just at the moment she was sliding into spinsterhood. At thirty-three she had fallen in love with a man who needed her every bit as much as she needed him. There were parallels between May and me that did not escape me.

Andy (on tricycle) and Bob in Albuquerque

In the summer of 1925, with the three children in the back of their uncertain Model T, Kyle and May took off on a tortuous rain-ridden journey, driving seventy miles over winding dirt roads and cattle trails in search of D. H. Lawrence. Kyle had written the controversial English novelist three times, asking for an interview, but never received an answer. Lawrence was said to be hiding in the Sangre de Cristo Mountains north of Taos, with his

German wife Frieda. With leads offered up by writer friends, that was where Kyle and May found him.

It must have been a curious meeting, the tall shy underweight would-be journalist and the scandalous novelist known for his sexually explicit writing and bawdy drawings. But the two men were kindred spirits. They were both sons of coal miners and tough-minded mothers, and they shared leftist political sentiments. And they both suffered from tuberculosis, the scourge of coal-mining communities. Lawrence would die of it just a few years later, in 1930.

Over a good deal of moonshine, Kyle and Lawrence spent their time together tearing into the growing materialism in the country and American commercial values. It was thanks to their genuine connection that Lawrence critiqued a story Kyle sent him a few weeks later, warning Kyle that "your visionary soul needs thawing":

> You are too journalistic, too much concerned with
> facts . . . I don't see why you shouldn't dig down in
> yourself 'til you get out of sight of your street self
> and there, little by little, get out the hidden stuff.
> You've got to allow yourself to be, in some
> measure, the mystic that your real self is, under all

the American efficiency and smartness of the ego—before you can be an artist.

Too little confidence, not enough money, too many children, an in-built shyness—God knows why—but Kyle wrote Lawrence that he didn't have the courage to become a creative writer. Kyle would go on to become a successful writer—the interview with Lawrence was a turning point—but he would always look over his shoulder before reaching for the hidden stuff. Even in his fiction, it never was, and never would be, expressed on paper except in letters to his children.

May didn't support much interior analysis, either. Raised by embittered parents, isolated by religion, she viewed introspection as a needless luxury. It was Bob who would search for the internal while Kyle stood on the sidelines, stuttering and cheering, providing money when money was needed.

Kyle had been raised Scotch Presbyterian, but became an agnostic and a leftist. May remained a Catholic. Neither of their families had been pleased about their marriage. Together they instilled a powerful confusion in their children. If the politics within their marriage was confusing, the tenor of their relationship was not. Theirs was a union of uncommon affection. For their forty years together, Kyle drove May to Mass every Sunday and sat in the car working the Sunday puzzle, chewing his cigar, keeping his own counsel, while waiting to take her home. One Sunday, the priest came out to the parking lot in an attempt to inveigle Kyle into attending mass. Kyle spluttered and waved his unfinished puzzle, the priest laughed and retreated, and the absurdity of the invitation became one of the family stories told and retold at cocktail time in Newtown.

On our walks in Newtown, Bob and I talked about religion, about ethics, about the comforts of tradition. I was a Jew but I had been brought up without religion. I longed for religion but remembered praying only once or twice. "I prayed the afternoon I lost my braces," I told Bob, "When I threw them out at school during lunch."

"You prayed when you lost your braces?"

"I couldn't go home without them. My father would have killed me."

And I begged God to let me say goodbye when my grandfather died. My grandfather Percy Lansburgh had always said that we were a pair. I believed him, not knowing what he meant. Just weeks before his death, we'd gone to the World's Fair with his other special friend, Tessie Grandago, who was young and dark and pretty. And then he died without warning.

The God I prayed to had no denomination but was a fragment drawn from random talk with maids and nannies and children in the park. God was the last hope for intercession and in my experience did not intercede. Being Jewish had nothing to do with God. As a child, being Jewish meant, as my grandfather explained it, that one could live at 875 Park Avenue but not at 890. *We* went to one country club, *they* went to another.

We lived among other Jews who pursued assimilation and didn't look too Jewish. Percy wore a smoking jacket and embroidered velvet slippers to dinner and spoke with the faintest touch of an English accent. We had Christmas trees with blue lights and dressed up for Easter, learned the psalms, read the Bible "as living literature," and followed in the steps of my great-great-grandfather, William Kraus, who wrote in 1900,

> I was brought up as an Israelite and I am still
> adhering to the old faith to a great extent. But as
> far as my personal views are concerned, I believe
> in most any of the religious matters if they carry
> out the doctrine of Christ who once upon a time
> was a Jew himself, and his doctrine was "You
> should do unto others as you would have others do
> unto you," and this is the biggest part of my
> religion today.

In 1942 I worked as a junior counselor at a summer camp in Boothbay, Maine. Looking forward to parents weekend, I booked a reservation for my mother and father at a small inn called the Oak Grove Hotel. Some days later, the reservation was rejected when the innkeeper recognized Feiner as a Jewish name. Antisemitism had seldom been a subject for family discussion. My father dismissed the incident in a letter:

> I know that you are disappointed at our not getting up to see you. So are we. I gather also that you are somewhat shocked and depressed at the reasons that have prevented our doing so. That however is a state of affairs which has been going on for some 12 or 15 hundred years. Remember, such things are not cured overnight. The phase which you have encountered (and which you will encounter many times again) is in terms of what is taking place elsewhere in the world.

> Personally I've never let it bother me because I find that it invariably occurs among people and organizations for whom I have nothing but contempt anyhow. This little Oak Grove place, for example, seemed to me like just the sort of mediocre, class C hotel that I never would have

chosen. If you learn to feel superior to such people —as you have every right to do—you'll find that the inconveniences which they may bring about are generally inconsequential.

I was a Jew because others said so. At Knox School where I was one of three Jewish girls, I refused to pray or bow my head at chapel. I was a Jew with friends who were Jews and from whom I tried to learn Yiddish phrases. And I was Jewish when I married a non-Jew. When I entered the Crichton family, I already ate ham and pork, worked on Yom Kippur and sang Christmas carols. But I slammed out of the room when someone slipped and used the word *kike*. I never admitted that both my grandmother and mother used the word as well in reference to those other kinds of Jews.

Kyle and I battled over the expression *Jew the man down*. Kyle insisted that beneath the vernacular, there was no ill will. I wanted to believe him but I wasn't sure. Then, at Thanksgiving dinner, with fourteen of us around the table, May asked what part of the turkey I would like. Without any hesitation, I asked for that great delicacy, the hind end of the bird, known in my family as *the Pope's nose*. May put down the carving knife and retreated to the kitchen. Bob turned pale and Kyle began to laugh.

That evening, after everyone went their separate ways, Kyle and I acknowledged we all had a lot to learn.

Bob was a Catholic who no longer believed. At Portsmouth Priory, the Catholic prep school where he had been sent to finish high school, he built a small shrine in his room with his classmate Robert Kennedy. He loved the rituals of the Church, the monks in their robes at the end of the day, moving over the lush Rhode Island hills singing Gregorian chants. During his months in combat, his vision of God shifted and Bob later wrote,

> He was a fox-hole God, an emotional God. One harrowing experience, a bloody attack and a heavy shelling finally brought God to me. I can say He walked by my side, that was the supreme emotional triumph. After the war, the experience could not be regenerated. Bit by bit, my God began to drop away.

But the Church and its ideals continued to pull at his heart. At the time we met, he was a supporter of Dorothy Day, the radical Catholic activist and leader of the Catholic Worker movement. Day was a Marxist, a Christian, a pacifist, and a glorious woman, and Bob was drawn to her blend of the spiritual and political.

On the days when the winds of idealism swept his soul, he would lambaste me for my materialist ways. "Would you still love me," he demanded, "if I became a shoe repairman?"

"I love you because you are you," I said, sidestepping the question.

CHAPTER 5

Bob's sense of time was as variable as he was. When the going was good he entertained an illusion that he could make time, break time, stretch time to his bidding. It might have come from the length of his stride; he could cover ground faster than anyone we knew. Friends from his childhood still called him Speedy. Even in winter, Bob wore sneakers—Jack Purcell sneakers. Bouncing slightly on the soles of his feet, he looked like a man about to enter an arena. A man's physical being revealed his character. He told our daughter Jennifer never to trust a man with a splay-footed gait. On the simplest errand, out to buy the morning paper, Bob moved down the street like a broken-field runner and turned corners sharply. But he was loose the way a dancer is loose, all of a piece, arms and hands and legs. In great part, he simply loved to move. He was still vaulting fire hydrants when he was over forty.

In the years right after the War, Bob was obsessed with time. The tenet of existentialism was the pacemaker within him. With death around the corner, there was nothing to do but live. He quoted Camus and Sartre: If this is all there is, then not an hour can be squandered. He wrote about the rootless aimless lonely restlessness around him. If death was inevitable, the unused life was the greatest sin. But no matter how fast he ran, there were too many diversions, too many people competing for attention. One entry in his diary is a stand-in for many.

> Wake up, my God, look at the time, Judy you must get up. My God, hurry buzzzz. I am shot, puffy eyed and generally unseeing, into clothes, out into hall, downstairs and then have a delightful time walking around to the Spanish, Italian, Assyrian etc. food stalls along Third Avenue. By the time I return the apartment is shining. A nice brunch and a nice talk until damn near 5. Can't say we weren't entertaining.

Bob was never just a host or just a guest, seldom a wanderer through someone else's life. The plumber would be asked to stay on for a drink. When we were still at 30th Street, our landlord's clerk, a shy young freckle-faced red-headed Black man known as Red would come for the rent and be lured into a discourse on the grace of Willie Mays. The simplest exchange was transformed into an event.

There was little quiet time that first winter we were together. Merging our lives was a complex business. We had an engagement almost every night and it was taking a toll.

Dec 26th, 1951
I worked on the book today and found it very hard going. It is much like athletics. A three or four day lay off is very hard indeed. Judy was tired at work today and I regret more than I can say that people are coming tonight.

Judy gets paid today and that is certainly good news. What would we do without a breadwinner in the house?

The Sunday after Christmas, we had a visit from Frank O'Hara and Lyon Phelps—two of the golden boys—which is how I thought of the Harvard literary pack that consisted of the poets O'Hara and Phelps, John Ashbery, Kenneth Koch, brilliant men all. They had met at Harvard just after the War, written for the *Advocate*, hung out at Eliot House and the Mandrake bookshop, rambled around with Edward St. John Gorey, Robert Bly, Donald Hall and Harold Brodkey, and, one memorable afternoon, sipped sherry with T. S. Eliot and E. M. Forster.

Bob was remembered as the undergraduate who had engaged Eliot and Forster in a three-way conversation.

Frank O'Hara with his strangely beautiful broken nose was already a star in New York. He was funny, acerbic and outrageously effeminate, and I never caught his eye. Lyon, still tightly locked in the closet, was a striking poetic beauty with long hair, more gentle and lonely than Frank, and I knew we would be friends. The three had met in Harry Levin's famed course on Joyce, Proust and Mann, the most demanding literature course at Harvard.

Bob served bloody Marys, I fixed brunch and hid my copy of *The Old Man and the Sea*. I knew enough to know that Hemingway was not up to their standards. That night, Bob wrote in his diary:

> Frank has now been accustomed to his series of
> little epigrams. He ceases to be able to talk or
> think successfully without hanging his thoughts
> on them. Did give one good description of a
> person as a wastebasket who will collect people
> indiscriminately.
>
> We had some fun talking about Edward St. John
> Gorey and Bob Bly who is working in New York

on his epical Indian saga (a Hiawatha with guts).
Phelps is looking ever more the image of Shaw's
poet in Candida. Women want to protect him and
he wants to be some man's woman, as I have on
one occasion seen.

I was as unfamiliar with homosexuals as I was with intellectuals. A friend said that Bob was "the only certified non-fairy in the group." It was a curious distinction and I wanted to know more but had neither the language nor the courage to even ask the many questions I had. Not so many years before, my friend Harriet had been drummed out of boarding school, dismissed for *having tendencies*. My mother was told that Harriet had been seen running her hand down my arm. The unforgiving headmistress, Mrs. Phinney, let me know that I had been in grave, if not mortal danger.

"Did you like Harriet?" Bob asked.

"I loved Harriet," I said, startled by my own answer.

Many of Bob's friends at Harvard were gay, but in that less easy age, he didn't notice or didn't seem to care. Lyon Phelps came back to 30th Street many times and later brought his parents. We were the straight friends he hoped would slake his mother's unspoken questions. He wrote a letter thanking us for our patience, for keeping "the terror of the big city from the door of my mind. I adore you both." But we never really provided the comfort that he needed. We were far too preoccupied with ourselves.

As Frank O'Hara and Lyon Phelps headed into the Village night, Bob and I raced off to an unusual party at Helga Trudeau's, an elegant middle-aged refugee with an Austrian accent and a pile of blonde hair high on her head. Helga drove a cab and lived in a rambling rent-controlled apartment on 86th Street between Park and Madison. (Her son Frank Conroy later chronicled his eccentric parents and their world in the cult classic *Stop-Time: A Memoir*.)

Dec 30th

We pulled ourselves together to go to Guy and Helga Trudeau's. They are cab drivers who have surrounded themselves with a group of Continentals, people in business, on the fringe of the arts, a psychoanalyst, a professor of government Arthur Schlesinger . . . Judy was surrounded by a group of admiring men like women are in parties in the movies (she looked very lovely), and we drank and danced.

On the way home we impetuously stopped to see
Vivien Leigh and Marlon Brando in Tennessee
Williams' Streetcar Named Desire.

We never did read one line of Shaw which makes
me feel a little restless, like Gide in The
Immoralist, which Judy knows.

We were like children now, racing in overdrive, high on adrenaline demanding more adrenaline. On New Year's Eve, after a full day's work, we went to three parties and the theater. Then just before dawn, we exploded.

At the stupid hour of 5 o'clock, both dead tired,
I begin a stupid argument which ends in a very
bad scene. I figure these things are always guilt
impulses of mine for wasting time . . . We are
both so tired and being nice to one another is at
times a great problem although we are easily
and obviously in love.

In the post-holiday exhaustion, I fought with my father Ben by transcontinental phone. That night Bob wrote in his diary:

Good bye, Daddy, Judy said and hung up in a frightful burst of tears. Her crying originally scared Ben into a realization of how far his neglect had alienated him and hurt others. Before, he had only to extend one smile and one pat a day on the heads of his children and they were content to hope for more.

A peculiar and well tried method about love is to be in a position to mete it out and never give quite enough. This will keep people wanting and waiting. They become satisfied with only a glance and work harder and harder to get the glance. The more they are shunned, the more they need. This is somewhat a truth in Judy's life.

Bob was right.

In 1945, the summer I was sixteen, my father packed up and left for Hollywood. My mother said it was a trial separation, and I didn't believe her. I had spent my childhood stalking my parents, hoping to catch any expression of affection. I marked their wedding anniversaries when they preferred to forget them. Then in the summer of 1946, my father was back and suddenly there was food in the refrigerator, placemats on the table. The overflowing ashtrays and desultory piles of unpaid bills all but disappeared. Mother looked almost pretty. She was tall and thin, with a long nose more Roman than Jewish, strong gray eyes, and a low voice made deeper by smoking.

But just hours after Ben's arrival, there was a dreadful fight, one of those loud mean name-calling spirit-destroying exchanges, quick stabs of hate and hurt escalating into charges and countercharges. My mother insisted she had taken other lovers. I knew she was lying and moved to intervene.

The following day, I called Dr. Jacobi, the alienist, psychiatrist, Freudian analyst who had treated my father for his addiction to sleeping pills at nighttime and uppers in the morning. In a family in which real talk was forbidden, everything I knew about my parents—what they thought about themselves or thought about each other, the downward spiral of our finances, their psychic health, the existence of Dr. Jacobi himself—I had learned from spying.

I was sixteen, a file clerk on *This Week* magazine, a Sunday supplement for *The Herald Tribune*. It was late in the morning when I called from the magazine to speak with Dr. Jacobi and told him that my parents were acting like children and I needed his help to keep them from getting a divorce. Dr. Jacobi lived and worked in a brownstone in the West 70s with a wide stoop and an engraved glass door. A housekeeper led me through a cool dark parlor in which the furniture had been covered for the summer with white sheets, the shades drawn against the summer sun.

Dr. Jacobi was tiny, far shorter than I, with a small goatee and thin white hair, a bust of Freud watching over his desk. He listened quietly as I told him the story and he handed me a tissue when I began to cry.

"Judy, I know you very well," he said when I had finished. "I've talked with your father and I've talked to your mother and now I want you to listen to what I have to say."

He paused. I waited.

"You must divorce your parents. Your father is a good man, but he's a child and he is selfish and he is not about to change. And your mother will hurt you for the rest of your life."

I lost my breath while Dr. Jacobi was talking. He did not seem concerned that I could not stop crying as he catalogued hurts I thought no one knew I had. But he also identified strengths.

"You are strong," he said. "You can lead a good life. You're a healthy girl. You can make it."

When the session was over, he put a hand on my shoulder and suggested I call him whenever I got frightened. I did so once or twice. He always said the same thing. Keep on going.

There was an old Jimmie Lunceford song Bob used to sing—*T'aint what you do, it's the way that you do it*—and that was what he was humming as we walked into Sardi's following the opening of the Rodgers and Hart revival of *Pal Joey*. I was out of sorts, having rushed from work only to arrive at the theater after the opening number. In my fractured family, Dorothy and Dick Rodgers held uncommon power, and one wasn't late for a Richard Rodgers opening.

When Dick Rodgers appeared on 44th Street, the waters all but parted. There probably wasn't a more celebrated Broadway figure alive than Dick. He'd composed the scores for 37 musicals and over a dozen films. *Oklahoma!* had become a national anthem, and the week *Pal Joey* opened, *South Pacific* and *The King and I* were still playing down the street to full houses. With my father's sister Dorothy as his perfect consort, Dick had been to Hyde Park for lunch with the Roosevelts and to Buckingham Palace for dinner with the Queen. Together they bought paintings by Matisse and Picasso. Dick was witty and generous. And every time I saw him, I found myself off-balance.

When Dick married my Aunt Dorothy, she was considered one of the most beautiful women in the country, pursued by Ronald Coleman and the Duke of Kent. She was a master of the elegant in art, food, clothes, in her posture that was both floating and upright, and in her soft, clear voice accented with the English-tinged pronunciation you used to hear in the movies. Called La Perfecta by Bennet Cerf and Princess by her father, Dorothy owned three ermine wraps by the time she was eighteen, and wore them wonderfully well.

Richard and Dorothy Rodgers

My father Ben, the brother of this magnificent obsessive, had grown up knowing he was the second-best child. To aggravate his insecurities even further, Dick Rodgers—his closest friend from childhood—was a recognized composer by the age of seventeen. My father was not without talent himself. He'd published three one-act plays while still in college but spent much of his adult life comparing himself to Dick. He lived and died, convinced he was a failure.

Every time my parents ran out of money, Dick threw them a lifeline. I grew up seduced by the Rodgers' glamour and was always on the defensive. I walked into Sardi's that night knowing I was on a family pass. But Bob didn't seem to care. He walked into Sardi's in his black tie and dress shirt, humming "T'aint what you do, it's the way that you do it." Settling down between Dick and the British actor Cedric Hardwick, Bob amiably began to talk about the War Book. I was seated between the *South Pacific* star Ezio Pinza and the movie star Kirk Douglas, and had absolutely nothing to say.

Bob knew he suffered the curse of charm. Our first winter together he wrote, "Each day I must watch and write down my progress on becoming a man instead of a man child." In a note to me he added:

I am glad we married young and feel a little sorry for those people who never had the chance to grow up with each other.

But he was wrestling with himself in our first year of marriage. It was clear there were too many empty-headed parties, too much drinking. In part it was my fault. I wanted everyone to meet the extraordinary man I'd married but had pushed it too far. I was living on thyroid pills, exhausted and jittery, and Bob was just plain played out. He talked about Scott Fitzgerald's bank of energy. Like Scott and Zelda, wed been drawing on our inner reserves and had little left.

We knew we were in trouble when on a Sunday morning we argued over whether I should have one piece of bacon or two. Mid-February, stalled on the War Book, Bob began writing magazine pieces. After being rejected by *The New Yorker*, he wrote in his diary:

I have utterly lost confidence in myself as a writer. When this happens, I have had the childish habit of waiting for some miracle to restore confidence. Judy knows then that I don't lead, I leave things all to her and this she doesn't like. I look for a mother then and she wants a father and this makes for a pretty insoluble situation.

Neither of us was prepared for the kind of marriage we were shaping and there were few templates. I was the breadwinner but he was head of household. He would decide where we went, who we saw, when we took a taxi, when we took a subway, how much money I could spend on a skirt. That's what husbands did, had always done. Just as a 19th-century mindset had shaped our thinking about war, it also influenced our attitudes towards each other and towards marriage.

I was a hybrid wife, domesticated but not domestic. I accepted that by virtue of Bob's superior intelligence—and by divine right of his being a man—he had been born to be boss. On the other hand, because he was home all day, I had little compunction leaving him the lion's share of the housework. Caught between the demands of daily life and his work, inevitably the work suffered. He left a letter for me at the office:

Because you have a job in the conventional sense,
your time has definite limitations. But I have a job
too and a very difficult one. Because I have my
own hours, concessions are often asked to be
waived.

The time I have has to be considered more important, the most important time around our house has got to be mine. Although I haven't written 10 famous books or 15 great musicals, I am that type of person.

Just as you don't expect those people to spend a great deal of their allotted time or wouldn't dream of asking them to, so do I rather aristocratically ask to be spared. I have an idea that they had the same feeling when they were young, only maybe they weren't quite so eager to be pleasant all the time. My ambition actually stumbles over that vice.

It was not an easy winter, for either of us.

One evening I came home from work, unkempt and out of sorts, to find my mother on our couch with a smooth and polished woman who drank Scotch and laughed at Bob's story about borrowing a tuxedo from a friend of his father's who had a withered arm. The fellow had died and Bob had been asked to return the suit for his burial.

I couldn't stand the way the woman with the well-kempt nails was laughing, the pleasure in Bob's eyes. I slammed together supper, my mother called me Doodle and lit another Lucky. Bob talked about the War, talked about his other self, the self that went into battle, leaving him safe behind. I was furious at his intimacy with this other woman, loathed the way she crossed her legs and locked his eyes. Around midnight as Bob left the apartment to escort her to a taxi, I watched as he put his hand on the small of her back, and went to bed in silence with my face against the wall.

As I dressed for work next morning, hungover with emotion, Bob put on real shoes and his crash linen jacket, brushed his hair too carefully, and headed for the door.

"Where are you going?" I asked. I knew he wouldn't answer. "Tell me where you're going."

He wouldn't say.

As he ran down the stairs, an air raid drill began and sirens shrieked their uneven wail. I ran after him but a warden interceded. As I reached Lexington Avenue, the warden chased me back into the house while Bob jumped into our car and drove away.

Ten hours later, after I'd spent a disorienting day writing publicity releases, Bob called collect from Jackson City. "Will you accept the call?" the operator asked.

I was serving supper to my friend Helen Marcus. I couldn't tell Helen that my husband was a scoundrel who had run off with a woman ten years older than he. I wouldn't reveal the capriciousness of our marriage. In a confusion of pride, with a fragment of Bob's voice echoing in my ear, I hung up the phone and went back to supper and our small talk.

But the moment Helen left, I called the long-distance operator and asked for Jackson City information. "Jackson City where?" asked the pleasant voice.

I said I wasn't sure but that I had to find my husband. In 1952 long-distance operators still had an air of adventure as they made connections, geographic and psychic. The operator suggested that if Bob had left New York in the morning, he might well have reached Jackson City, Tennessee by night. There were three hotels in Jackson City, she told me. Bob wouldn't stay at the most expensive, that much I knew. "He won't be at the cheapest either," the operator said. So she rang the hotel in the economic middle and I could hear her voice as she asked the desk clerk if a Robert Crichton was registered. And then, Robert Crichton was on the phone.

Later he described lying on the bed, alone and confused, reading the hotel room's Bible in a town where no one knew him, when suddenly he was jolted back to himself by the ringing of the phone. It was, he said, like the hand of God. He could barely reach for the receiver. But he did, and it was me, and I was crying.

"I'll come right home," he said, and he arrived late the following morning.

"Did she go with you to Tennessee?"

"Only to Washington. I took her to her parents, her father was an admiral, we talked about the War and then I headed south."

"Why did you go off?"

"I'm not sure," he answered.

Within years, we told the story together, elaborating on the wonder of my tracking him down. Hurt and confusion were ironed out of each retelling but never completely erased the questions in my mind.

I tried to sift between fact and fancy. Fact was, he loved me, maybe. Fact was, he didn't always come home. Fancy was, the stories he told me when he didn't. Maybe those stories were true. And maybe they were not.

No matter what anyone may say, no matter how
badly I may act. No matter how awfully you may
act I am always and hopelessly in love with you.
RCC

Viv, Andy, Billy and Bob in Albuquerque

Bob was mixing a martini in a battered silver shaker that had been my mother's when he first told me about his younger brother Billy. We were standing in the kitchen of our 30th Street apartment, smaller than a closet, with yesterday's dishes in the stained and dirty sink. This man with whom I lived on such an intimate basis, with whom I'd shared every detail of my own life, began talking about a brother I had never heard of before, a brother who had been erased from Crichton history.

This is what Bob knew about his little brother: May had been over forty when Billy was born. Billy was always odd and developed such a temper, he could no longer be kept at home. Billy was sent to live with a family on Long Island.

"Was he retarded?" I asked.

"I think so," Bob said.

"Did he look different?"

He couldn't remember.

No one ever gave Billy's problem a name. But when Billy was eight, in 1938, his dog ran onto elevated railroad tracks in Garden City, Billy ran after the dog, and both Billy and the dog were killed by the third rail. (The full story, told in the clipping below from *The Brooklyn Eagle*, was even more gruesome.)

Writer's Son Dies Trying to Save Dog

Garden City Park, June 14—While attempting to rescue his dog, wedged beneath the third rail, William Crichton, 8-year-old son of Kyle Crichton, magazine writer, was killed here yesterday by a westbound Long Island train near the Denton Ave. bridge.

With the engineer, George Septhon of Bay Head, unaware of the accident, the boy's body was dragged 50 feet to the bridge, where it dropped through the ties and was found by Fred Rothstein, a passerby. The dog, a white American bull named Puddles, was electrocuted.

Young Crichton boarded with Matthew Frontas of Atlantic Ave., Garden City. The elder Crichton lives at 60 Summit Ave., Bronxville.

The Crichtons were living in Bronxville, a leafy suburb just outside New York, when Kyle and May received the news, and they left for Long Island without talking to their children about what had happened. The following morning, Bob, Viv and Andy went to school and it was there they learned of Billy's death for the first time. By then, Kyle was a well-known magazine writer and editor, and *The Brooklyn Eagle* headline read, "Writer's Son Dies Trying to Save Dog." After school, over Andy's objections, Bob went out for a baseball game. His coach and teammates called him brave, but Bob knew better. Bob was on the run.

The Crichtons had moved to Bronxville a few years earlier when Kyle was making an astonishing amount of money writing two and sometimes three articles a week for *Collier's* magazine. From the dusty Western outpost of Albuquerque to the mean streets and parochial school in Jackson Heights that Bob depicted in his unfinished *The Minnow Fishers* to the exclusive world of WASPy Bronxville: it was an unlikely trajectory for the Crichtons.

Yet here they settled in The Boulders, a Tudor-style mansion atop a steep, winding driveway, with a living room large enough for basketball, a walk-in fireplace and bookcases that rose to the ceiling. Bob claimed he could play drums at one end of the house without those at the other end ever hearing.

The family story was that the day they moved in, a neighbor rang the bell to welcome May to Bronxville: "This is such a lovely community," she said. "You will be pleased to know we have no Negroes, no Jews, not even any Italians." The rest of the story, when told by Bob, was that May flashed back, "Well, isn't that too goddamn bad." But that line probably is from the realm of "what should have been said." The children had arrived in Bronxville as outsiders and remained outsiders until the day they left.

Bob began hanging out on the wrong side of town with what his brother Andy called "the wooden nickel crowd," and after Bob's freshman year of high school, May and Kyle sent him off to Portsmouth Priory, the only Catholic prep school modeled along the lines of the classic Protestant ones. But Bob returned to Bronxville often enough to rack up a slew of stories about drinking and girls and driving cars too fast around dead-man curves on back roads. My own stories tended to be variations on a theme, told from the inside out. But Bob seemed to stand on the outside of his life looking at himself with a curious kind of remove, almost as if he were a character in one of his own stories.

Talking about his teenage years, he mentioned that during his Bronxville days he'd been fingered as a car thief. "When I was eighteen, in one of those villages in Westchester, they accused me of stealing six cars. I want to get it straight right now. I didn't take one car. I took no car at all. Even though some of the circumstances are suspicious and my family still thinks that I did, along with all my friends." At a cocktail party in the early 1980s, our daughter Sarah met a man from Bronxville who told her, "I remember your father—he was the chap who stole all those cars." But we will never know the truth of it.

Years after Bob told me about Billy, I found an old steamer trunk in the Newtown attic filled with hundreds of Crichton snapshots, and photos that had been clumsily chopped to excise the offending Billy. But one surviving Kodak revealed four handsome children, blonde and smiling, looking very much alike.

My father Ben, who was able to define the differences between a Communist, a Fellow Traveler, a Sympathizer and a Lefty with all their subtle variations, flew in from Hollywood and took me to lunch. In a quiet corner of the Barberry Room in the old Berkshire Hotel, he raised a question he had been edging towards ever since the night he and Kyle first met: Was Kyle now, or had he ever been a member of the Communist Party? In the 1950s, Communist was a word you didn't hear in restaurants like the Barberry Room, with linen and crystal and self-assured businessmen at many-course lunches.

I bristled at the question and didn't know the answer. It was clear that that the government considered Kyle a Communist. Kyle had been under suspicion and sometimes under surveillance since the 1930s. No one disputed that he was a leftist. While working as a staff writer for *Collier's* magazine, Kyle had contributed to the Communist weekly, *The New Masses*, under the pseudonym of Robert Forsythe. But that was all I knew.

The distinction between a card-carrying member of the Party and a Fellow Traveler seemed extremely important. Years later Bob wrote, "In the days of the Great Depression my father turned to the left for ways to save a society he saw coming apart around him. I don't know if he ever joined the Communist party; I never asked him. I never met anyone who knew him who thought he had."

Kyle's leftist bent was a direct product of the social injustice he saw all around him in the coal camps of Pennsylvania and West Virginia and as the son of Scottish immigrants who believed in the promise of America. Kyle questioned whether capitalism could ever lead to peace and justice but he had always been a passionate American.

1952 was a dangerous time for anyone who had ever questioned the system. The world felt polarized—us against them. The Soviets had tested their second atom bomb, the United States was countering with the H-bomb, and many believed Korea was the opening battle in a third World War. Newtown took on an unhealthy quiet. Even cocktail time was muted. Kyle drifted from one overstuffed chair to the next, unable to concentrate even on the newspapers. On the flimsiest of charges—often no charges—government workers, army officers, school-teachers were accused of being Russian spies. We

Target: *Kyle Crichton was harassed by the F.B.I. and the House Un-American Activities Committee for over a decade. When one interrogation was over, "the humiliation of inquisition by incompetents would begin again."*

My Father, the Un-American

By Robert Crichton

"...The idea that agents of his government were coming to my father's house to question his loyalty made him sick to his soul..."

Bob's March 10, 1975, article in New York magazine

scanned the papers daily, fearful that Kyle's name would appear on the lists of unAmericans, those accused of being traitors. It was absurd. And it was terrifying.

In early July, Bob's mother May asked us to come to Newtown for the weekend. Mr. Jackson Jones, an investigator for the House UnAmerican Activities Committee, was arriving that Sunday to talk to Kyle. "Some disturbing things," Jones said, "had floated up from the files." From the day May and I first met, I knew that she was tough. But I never understood just how tough she could be until I saw how she marshaled all her forces when Jackson Jones arrived in Newtown to interrogate her husband.

Bob described Jones's visit in "My Father, the Un-American," a piece he wrote for *New York* magazine in 1975:

> Mr. Jones wasn't at all what we expected. He arrived a little after noon on Sunday, rather plump and pink, with thinning blond hair, a flamingo pink Cadillac convertible with the top down. To make a solid impression on Mr. Jones, my mother had invited all of the rock-ribbed Republicans, all the Thoroughly Respectable we knew, for drinks. Pillars of society.
>
> Pillars or not, they liked to start their drinking early, and before we were through trivia time with Jackson Jones, the room was filled with tweeds and button-down Brooks Brothers shirts, regimental ties and salt-and-pepper hair. The cocktail noise welled up the way it does when gentiles gather in exurbia and get their drinks.
>
> One has to hand it to Jones. He had a sense of theater. At the right moment, he managed to

signal that the time had come, and the room fell almost silent as my father threaded his way through the Good People and into a downstairs bedroom like a boy heading into the headmaster's office to face expulsion. People watched the door close and then they looked at the leather suitcase Jones had left on the coffee table.

Judge Boyle, the good conservative Republican Boyle who May knew from church, put his finger to his lips and pointed at the briefcase which Jones had left behind. For an hour we directed all our small talk to that briefcase which everyone assumed contained a hidden microphone. May passed the cheese dip, Bob refilled glasses, and at last Kyle and Jackson Jones emerged from their meeting in the bedroom. Kyle looked drained and Jones was hungry. May made him a sandwich and soon we heard Jones say in his cozy Southern way, "Be going down to New York, now, anyone wanting a ride, I'll be pleased to take them."

May responded, "Well, isn't that nice. Bob and Judy would love a ride."

It was a loathsome idea but May left us no choice. "You're going to get in that car, and be so charming and so wonderful and so understanding, you can't stand yourself." And we were.

We all crammed into the front seat of the Cadillac, me wedged between Jackson Jones and Bob, and we set out for the City. Bob was quieter than I had ever known him. I could feel the trembling in his thigh. We reached the Westside Highway and, as Bob wrote, "the city was blanketed in that velvet of late evening which seems to belong to New York more than to any city I know."

The day was over, and yet it wasn't. There were surprises in store. Although we lived on 30th Street, Jones turned off the highway on 79th Street and headed for the East Side. We parked near York Avenue, across from a massive new apartment building.

"Abe Burrows lives there. Going to have to close that man's show down."

"For what?" Bob was close to shouting.

"Man's a Communist."

"Who said so?"

"Oh, come on," Jones said, with a look of quiet surprise. "Everyone knows that. He's been named."

Bob suggested he couldn't close a show down just because someone said a man was a Communist.

"House Un-American Activities can."

Bob was moving onto dangerous ground but either Jones didn't notice or didn't care. He was on a roll now, a soft, pudgy man with incomprehensible power. We were captives on his tour bus, our smiles fixed and frozen, as

Jackson Jones drove around the city, pointing out the homes of well-known traitors who would never work again: Lillian Hellman, Betty Comden, Marc Blitzstein, Adolph Green, Zero Mostel. How easily the word *traitor* slipped off his tongue.

Later that night Bob said he had learned what Brecht meant when he said it was terrible to live in a country where it was forbidden to laugh but it was hell to live in a country where you were required to.

When Jones finally dropped us off at our apartment on 30th Street, he insisted Bob meet him at the Waldorf the following day. He wanted to talk about the possibility of doing a story on some Central European who had crashed through the Iron Curtain. Bob had no option. As he described it,

> When I got there, Jones had a rather skimpy
> manuscript, but he wasn't really interested in it.
> Why did he want me here? We had nothing to say
> or share. Now I think I know why.

> Here he was for a few short months from small-
> town Georgia in his suite in the Waldorf-Astoria:
> room service at the flick of a finger, a power to be
> reckoned with, a dangerous man, representing one
> of the most powerful and dangerous investigative

bodies ever unleashed on America by its Congress, and he was lonely, he had no one to share it with. It is, after all, the very stuff American dreams are made of.

The following weekend, Bob and I were back in Newtown. There was one and only one elliptical reference to Jones, and then the subject was closed. We never learned what Kyle and Jones had talked about, sequestered in the downstairs room, and FOIA requests for documents about Kyle have come up short. But it was clear Kyle was worried about money in his blacklisted state. Bob tentatively raised the issue, and Kyle responded a few days later with this note:

Dear Bob:

A word about our financial philosophy: we have some money saved up and when we run short in the checking account we cash another bond. The magazines seem closed to me but we've stopped worrying about it. If necessary we'll spend what we've saved and then head for the County Home. I'm not joking. We've decided it will be that way and my mind is completely at ease about it.

But starvation is at least ten years in the future and in the meantime the hell with it. So enjoy yourself, the cobalt bomb may never be used.

I thought we had a particularly good weekend.

Pop

The government never returned to Newtown. We will never know if Jackson Jones decided Kyle was not worth pursuing or if Kyle's brothers, now wealthy businessmen in Tennessee and Pennsylvania with political clout, managed to reach the chairman of the House Committee. But there was never an all-clear. No declaration that the inquisition was finally over. Once on the disloyal list, one remained on it forever.

CHAPTER 8

For one brief spell, we both tried to freelance, sitting at opposite ends of the large room we lived in, striving to work in a companionable fashion. Talk about the absurd. Bob put up a string across the middle of the room declaring we would not talk or hold each other while the string was in place. The string came down so often, I went out to look for a proper job, leaving him alone to wrestle with the War Book.

My absence didn't free him. I would come home after work and search for proof of progress. All I found were fragments and a 3x5 card which said:

The frustration of the artist lies in his ability to
perceive the ideal and in his inability to achieve it.
He exists as a failure to himself.
RCC

We were always broke, borrowing money, juggling creditors. The landlord's clerk Red was no longer sent to collect our rent. His boss came instead and was far less forgiving. On a miserably hot Sunday morning in August,

Bob and I left Newtown early to attend a dress rehearsal of a new Broadway musical, *Wish You Were Here.* The ambitious production, featuring a full-sized swimming pool, was based on Arthur Kober's *New Yorker* stories about a summer resort in the Catskills. I was a junior publicist assigned to write a short feature about the rehearsal, and Bob elected to keep me company.

We were sitting alone at the back of the theater when in the middle of the first act, the revolving platform designed to convey the swimming pool onto the stage came to a shuddering halt. While stagehands struggled with the mechanism and chorus girls in two-piece bathing suits climbed out of the pool, an overbearing stink began to drift through the house. The staff dispersed throughout the theater trying to find the source of the ripe, dank, putrid stench, and to my horror, I discovered it was rising from a sack of cow manure ripening at Bob's feet. Bob had brought the manure down from Connecticut to feed our anemic house plants. This was not a commercial product purchased from a nursery, sanitized and deodorized for domestic consumption. This was the real stuff, collected from a neighboring farm in Newtown.

As aides began to comb the theater, Bob slipped out to the street lugging his offending parcel while I followed nattering in embarrassment and fury. Back at our apartment, I made it clear that he would have to choose between the cow manure and me. Without hesitation he grabbed the burlap sack, raced out into the hall and shoved the offending parcel down the incinerator chute.

Three hours later, when the building's unsuspecting super began to burn the trash in the basement, smoke began to fill the building's stairwell and sifted under the doors of every apartment. The sack of manure had not made it down the incinerator chute after all, but had somehow caught fire and continued to smolder for hours. As puzzled tenants, coughing and choking, were driven out onto the street, Bob promised to give up organic gardening in the city.

At night we went back to self-analysis. Bob wrote in his diary that I wanted to know more about him and he wanted to understand more about himself. We combed his childhood trying to analyze those forces that were holding him back and became obsessed by the line between neurosis and madness. "How do you define madness?" he asked. Neither of us was certain.

We had begun to accept that in some way the War had changed the chemistry within him. But we never discussed it with the outside world. Andy later said that when Bob came home from Europe, his mind was "a wick's length away from exploding." Few knew how edgy

Bob was. He was tall, engaging: Big Bob Crichton, ebullient Bob who snapped his fingers with the speed and clarity and rhythm of Gene Krupa did not appear to be a man on the edge of a breakdown. But more often than I wanted to admit, Bob was in danger of losing his footing.

In November 1953 I received this letter:

Judy darling:

I have to tell you something which takes all my heart and strength to tell you . . . For the past several months (it really must be years) I have been going through a period in which I might very well have lost my mind or my way.

I think you of all people, by your wonderful belief and courage, have finally helped me get the courage to honestly put my life in perspective where it belongs.

Thinking of having a child has again made me reexamine. I really never did think of having one til some mysterious time when we would be in position to have one. The way I was going that would be never.

I know I have disappointed you terribly in many ways. Now I want to ask you to have all the courage you can possibly summon and believe in me.

While I was writing *The Minnow Fishers*, I often got terrible fears that I was losing my mind and as time passed and I became a stutterer who had lost nearly all his nerve entirely I knew I had to face something sooner or later and didn't know what it was. But I did know that my progress was causing you and me the most brutal type of torment.

It led me to lie and it led me to be ashamed. It made me bottle up my love for you because I felt I wasn't worthy . . . When I once left you for a little while it wasn't another woman but it was that I felt I had used up all my tricks and well meaning intentions and that you were beginning to see the shallowness of the skeleton that lay beneath.

I want to start over on the war book because I have to. I can only say that you must believe in me now more than ever. You will find it hard to believe that I thought of everything including staging a fire to get rid of the thing. But the book is not right. It is bad and it is dishonest. I can write the thing and I can write it swiftly. I have lived with it in my mind for these many months and years.

The letter charted hard days. But all I really absorbed was that Bob loved me and we were having a baby.

When I was six months pregnant, Bob asked a photographer named Homer Page to take my portrait. The photograph is surprisingly sober: my hair pulled back in a knot, my hands resting beneath my stomach. The girl is gone but Bob loved that picture. The baby had become the central focus of our life.

We moved into the second floor of a 19th-century house on a tree-lined street in Greenwich Village. The staircase was aslant, the rooms small and square but the leftover bits of molding around the doors and windows reassured Bob who had come to loathe the clean blonde Swedish good taste modern decor that accompanied so many of our friends into marriage. The living room opened onto a wooden deck which ran across the back of the house, one corner graced by the shade of a tall ailanthus tree.

Photograph by Homer Page;
I was 23 years old

Bob installed window boxes of geraniums and ivy and, in time, a sandbox on the deck—our outdoor room, he called it. Evenings, he'd throw a ball through Upstairs Irma's window and our new friend Irma would come downstairs to join us for a drink on the deck.

Bob was now going out to work every day. He had a desk in the office of friends and was writing magazine articles by the pound, "hack work," he called it. He wrote for *Argosy* and *True* and *Cavalier* magazines about piranha fish with a lust for destruction, about inept British noblemen who led barely-trained soldiers into the Valley of Death during the Crimean War, and about the pride, vanity and lust for glory that had driven George Armstrong Custer into a tragic blunder. That piece raised all kinds of hell.

I had been hired as a researcher by Allan Sherman, a wonderfully idiosyncratic little man, to find the "secrets" for his benign television game show, *I've Got a Secret.* (Allan Sherman would later be best known for his novelty hit, "Hello Muddah, Hello Fadduh.") The pay was good and we lived on it for years. Bob was amused by the absurdity of my work. Over my years on the show, I reunited Louis Armstrong with his first trumpet teacher, found the man who pushed a peanut up Pike's Peak with his nose, and on one memorable afternoon, wrestled with a curator in fishing boots in the basement of the Aquarium as he tried to kiss me on a wet and slimy floor covered with a coven of live electric eels. The spring of 1954, when I was pregnant with Sarah, a large and friendly boa constrictor wrapped around my ankles during an *I've Got A Secret* rehearsal. I fainted and Bob cooked supper for us both that night. It was lovely to be pregnant with Bob in the spring time.

Perry Street was the sweetest time in our life. It was here the first three children were born—Rob a year and a half after Sarah, and Jenny just a year after Rob: Irish twins, Bob called them. Three cribs were jammed into a room the size of a closet. When we opened the door in the morning, the smell of ammonia was overwhelming but the children were there with outstretched arms and all seemed right with the world. Bob carried them all like sacks of potatoes tucked beneath his arms, sang them songs of his own devising, and learned to balance a basketball on his finger to lure them away from the television set. Early childhood development became an obsession. We listed every word the children learned and charted their precocities.

When Sarah was born, Bob gave me a pink geranium and said I was beautiful and brave and that he loved me the more. I had never held an infant in my arms. Bob had had some practice with nieces and nephews. But Sarah was tough and sunny and clear about her desires, and I was startled to discover just how much I loved her. My grandmother Mae Feiner came for dinner and watched me change the baby. "We never had to do that," she told Bob in disgust. The Feiners had nannies and nannies who replaced the nannies on their days off. The Feiners also alienated their children and that was not our intent. We followed Dr. Spock into the world of hands-on childcare and firm but empathetic discipline.

On the Perry Street deck

On an August night when I was rocking Sarah to sleep, a clutch of young people stopped beneath our bedroom window. I could hear them laughing and flirting and for a moment I was wistful for the life I would never have again. I was only 24 myself. And then I turned and found that Bob, the baby and I were lying on our bed enveloped in a kind of peace I'd never known before.

Rob was enormous and an easy infant, more interested in eating and later in climbing, than in learning to talk.

A snapshot at a year and half catches him standing on the kitchen counter with a box of crackers in his hand. He walked like Bob and stood like Bob and even put his hand on his hip like Bob. Jennifer was the most sensitive and for the first months of her life slept apart from the others in a laundry basket we placed in the bathtub.

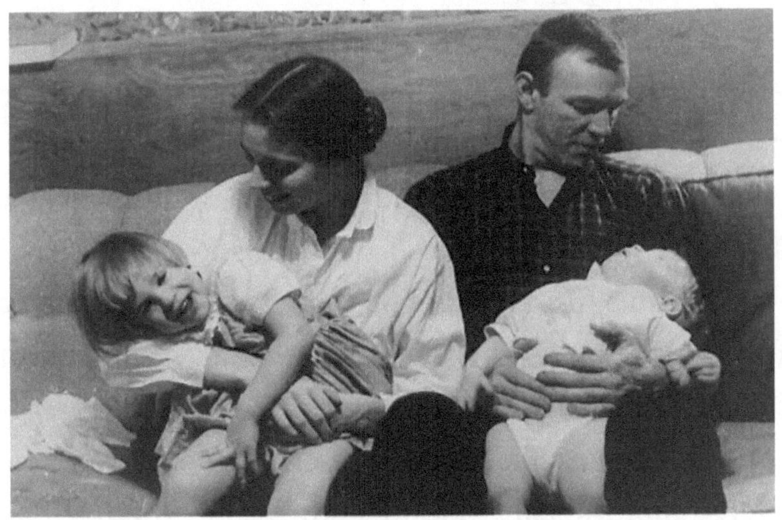

With Sarah and Rob

God, we were proud and Bob so loved his birds: our strong, confident, bright-eyed children. The furies of the earlier years had lessened, he seldom lost his temper, the war dreams subsided. My family was appalled by my fecundity but we were amused. The debris of childhood filled the house. At the end of every day, Bob came home and reinvented the apartment.

The bad times: we managed to forget them. Disasters became stories and stories became legends. More often than not, we ran out of money. After every baby, I would be forced back to work. We would hire a sitter and Bob would convince the editor of *Argosy* to forget all the reasons he was no longer on staff. He continued to be hired and fired on a regular basis.

The final time Bob was fired from *Argosy* was just before Christmas 1957. The children and I were already ensconced in Newtown. Bob was coming up by train with a pink slip in his pocket and the last-minute presents I asked him to buy including a rubber baby doll for Sarah. Over martinis in a favorite bar, distressed he'd been let go once again, Bob let the Christmas packages slip beneath his feet. On the train to Danbury, three or four martinis down, he tried to pull the presents together and discovered that the baby doll was now filthy—trampled and smudged. With the last vestiges of responsibility left within him that day, Bob took the rubber baby into the men's room of the train, peeled off her dress, petticoat and bloomers, and began to give her a proper bath in the tiny lavatory sink.

When the conductor opened the door in a routine search for deadbeats, he found Bob with a cigarette dangling from his mouth, shirtsleeves rolled up, soaping Sarah's doll in the small steel sink, singing a Christmas carol as he did. The conductor took a look, closed the door, and moved along. Bob arrived in Newtown with his ticket unpunched, the baby doll for Sarah and yet another story for Christmas Eve.

Bob on the Perry Street deck, photo taken from Upstairs Irma's

On the deck with Sarah and Rob, and Upstairs Irma

Our world seemed composed of contrasts and extremes. Upstairs Irma never forgot the evening when she came downstairs to sit for us so that we could head off to the Rodgers' 25th anniversary party at the Pierre. Bob had put on a beautifully tailored tuxedo and looking dashing, hit her up for taxi money before we left. Marilyn Monroe was promised to be among the many stellar guests. Monroe had arrived late—she was always late—wearing one of her signature black dresses with spaghetti straps. She stood by herself at the edge of the dance floor—watching, waiting—her mouth slightly open. A hundred men in the room longed to join her but didn't, but then Bob was at her side and the waiters and the busboys and the cooks from the kitchen and Averell Harriman and Adlai Stevenson formed a circle round the dance floor and Monroe was in Bob's arms, and they were dancing.

It is curious to be the wife of a man who is holding Marilyn Monroe—the fantasy so alive, too alive, Monroe so round, her arms so soft. Bob was far more circumspect than usual. Ordinarily he was an outrageous dancer who would lope and strut, do the boogie-woogie, the Hesitation and the Shuffle, steps he'd learned hanging out in the Harlem Ballroom before the War, whip his partner back and forth. He was the first man I knew who danced with or without music and loved to dance alone. But Marilyn set the tone, and Bob kept his hand on her waist, not too high, not too low. He was talking, she was laughing, and then John Hersey, quiet gentle John, the great writer of *Hiroshima*, a missionary's son, tapped Bob on the shoulder and danced Marilyn away. And we went home to Perry Street and tried to scrounge up the money to pay Irma back.

Bob needed a book idea and that idea was Ferdinand Waldo Demara, a man the *New York Times* called the most agreeable impostor of our time. Bob would write his story for his first book, *The Great Impostor,* and the small advance from Random House seemed at first to be a godsend.

When we first met Fred Demara in 1956, he looked like an amiable linebacker gone soft: too vivid a man to be a successful fake, it would seem, though no one had ever been a better one. While most impostors steal credentials, Demara stole entire lives, then lived them fully and successfully until he was unmasked or got bored and gave himself away. A high school dropout, he had passed himself off as a college dean, a Doctor of Philosophy, a zoologist, a prison warden and once, driven to extremes, as the auditor for a Texas hotel. As a Catholic Brother, he retreated to monasteries in ten states, then moved on to con yet another kind-hearted abbot. During the Korean War, Demara joined the Canadian Navy as a surgeon named Dr. Joseph Cyr.

When nineteen badly wounded Koreans were carried aboard his ship, Demara successfully cleaned, probed and sutured their wounds with instruments he had never held before. All the men were said to have survived. Although he was depicted as a jolly Walter Mitty, Fred was in fact one of the loneliest of men who smiled on command, seldom out of desire. He would loll around our house, a big fat restless know-it-all, overly solicitous and demanding at the same time.

When the world caught up with Demara and he was forced back into his own skin, he'd go off on suicidal binges. Shortly after he agreed to work with Bob, he holed up in a two-bit West Side hotel and drank himself to the brink of death. Bob dragged him off to Bellevue, not at all sure that Fred would pull through. But Demara had the constitution of an ox, and within three days he managed to persuade a staff psychiatrist that he was a physician, not a patient.

To try to unlock Fred's psyche and apply some psychological order to his rambling tales, Bob and Demara went out on the road, back to the scenes of his previous capers. It was an extraordinary trip: Bob the fantasist, and the Great Impostor drinking, fighting and lying to each other as they worked together to keep our dying car alive. The Deathwagon, Bob called it. Bob was so fearful that Fred would run away, he hardly ever let the man out of his sight. His calls home were brief and unrewarding.

Sarah was two, Rob one, I was pregnant with Jennifer, and we were broke, always broke. The book advance barely financed the road trip. We had borrowed from everyone we knew and in anger and embarrassment, I finally called Kyle for help. This was his response, along with a generous check:

Dear Judy:

Don't worry about it; the book will be done some
day and I think you'll make money out of it. Right
now things seem to be piling up but there will be
an end to them and you must realize that if Bob
can get that Sat Post assignment when every writer
in the country is trying to break in there, he really
is in a good position. He'll pop out on top one of

these days and be there for a long time.

The business of the lies, even the white lies, is not good for him, but he does it out of a desire not to hurt people. On a matter of principle he never wavers a bit. Your marriage is an instance of that. So, heads up and the stiff lip and all that sort of thing. You'll come through.

Love,

Kyle

The night Bob came home, his arms were filled with dirty clothes and books, including a well-thumbed copy of *Why You Do What You Do,* and a dried-up cotton plant he had picked for Sarah. Fred had not been an easy traveling companion and Bob was exhausted. As I was serving up the pork chops, he slipped on a toy and fell against the edge of our marble-topped table. We made little of the moment. He was drinking and I was going into labor.

Around two in the morning, I woke Bob to say the time had come to go to the hospital, he declared with some irritation that he was suffering a massive heart attack and for several minutes we argued over who was in greater extremis. Upstairs Irma came down to stay with the children, Bob was bleary-eyed and groaning, and I was bracing against the next contraction as we made our way out onto 7th Avenue to find a cab.

At New York Hospital, Bob was led in one direction, I in another, two wheelchairs passing in the night. About an hour later, he joined me in the labor room breathing slightly easier. He had broken two ribs when he fell against the table. His heart was fine, his chest was taped and moments later our baby was born. As her red hair was being dried, Bob began to sing, "Oh, will you wear red, oh my dear, oh my dear, will you wear red, Jenny Jenkins? I won't wear red, it's the color of my head . . ." Then, having named our baby, he placed Jenny in my arms and left to go home to take care of our other birds. Now we were five.

Bob was working hard on *The Great Impostor* and for a few months, I was a full-time mother with three children under two and a half. The yellow shag rug we had inherited from our friends, the Bartles, turned an unwholesome mustard color.

"Brush your hair," Bob said.

"I will," I answered, warming yet another bottle.

He had a brief flirtation with a dark-haired woman. My Aunt Jane—my mother's sister, as bitter and unkind as my mother was—told me she had seen them drinking wine in the Village. Bob was rotten, yes. We hadn't been out to dinner together for the length of a lifetime. Too many babies, too little money. He was contrite, particularly about the dinner. In his copy of Emerson's *Conduct of Life,* he underlined "Poverty demoralizes." But I was less forgiving than I'd been in the past.

We had grown out of the Village apartment on quiet tree-lined Perry Street we both loved so well. When we had left 30th Street, we never looked back. That apartment has been just one step up from an adolescent crash pad, a training ground for marriage with unfinished slipcovers. But Perry Street was home. The morning the movers came for our move to Morningside Heights, I sat on the stoop under the shade of a ginkgo tree with Jennifer in my arms, and Sarah and Rob sitting beside me.

The Village was a real village. Sarah, not yet three, could run to the corner fruit store for a quart of milk and a chat with our friends who ran the place. The minister from across the street would settle in for long conversations with Bob while Bob was sweeping the stoop. It wasn't Bob's to sweep, of course, but he loved the look of the building once it was all tidy. The day before we moved, we'd gone to say goodbye to our friends in Washington Square Park. We promised we would bring the children back to visit, knowing full well we likely never would.

CHAPTER 10

W e moved to an apartment in a new brick jungle on the edge of Harlem. On the surface, Morningside Gardens was everything Bob loathed: a faceless urban village of several thousand people, six twenty-one-story buildings, Orwellian in their tidiness with every door and knob alike. The rooms were light but charmless, security guards patrolled the grounds, and a co-op rulebook codified every aspect of our communal existence: no laundry on the balconies, no running in the halls, no playing ball on the grounds after six.

But beneath the bureaucratic imperatives, Morningside Gardens was unique. It was an interracial community and that was rare in the 1950s. Most of us white people had spent our lives in one-color worlds. Physically New York was as segregated as the South, not by law but by social fiat: a mindset as arbitrary as a whites-only sign on an Alabama men's room. 125th Street was the city's demarcation line. As a kid, Bob had wandered uptown to the jazz clubs to hear Willie "the Lion" Smith, Fletcher

Henderson and Dizzy Gillespie, but I had never had that sense of adventure.

We were an eclectic group of tenants at the Gardens, self-selected, to be sure. It was a haven for unreconstructed activists: Marxists and socialists, feminists and integrationists. The 60s really began in the 50s. It was a strange bifurcated time. The Howdy-Doody, Captain Kangaroo postwar world of Reader's Digest happiness collided with arguments over human relations and the politics of race, Communism and the growing fear of atomic annihilation. In school, children were taught to duck and cover when the bombs began to fall. Bob was enraged by the suggestion that a child could find safety from a nuclear war by crouching beneath a school desk. "Tell that to the parents of the children at Hiroshima," he would say.

There was more talk about sex in these days with the Kinsey Report, Elvis, Lolita, and Norman Mailer all expanding the vision of what was socially acceptable. A couple on the 19th floor of our building were followers of Wilhelm Reich and owned an orgone box which looked like a phone booth and was said to release one's sexual powers. The FDA declared the box a fraud and Reich was put in jail. But true believers were not deterred by government edicts.

I was appointed to the Gardens' co-op board where we fought out social issues on a weekly basis. At an early meeting, a Black lawyer insisted we needed additional play areas within our protected enclave. I argued that his older children could use the neighboring playgrounds over in the projects. With some edge to his voice, he said I was confusing race and class, that in the world beyond the Gardens, his children were as vulnerable as mine, their darker skin offering no protection against local thugs. I was embarrassed and knew that he was right. I was an integrationist who had yet to shed racism or understand the extent to which it shaped my thinking. As a child I had been taught the intricacies of class, to place everyone I met into a complex social narrative. All the clues had changed. The lawyer and I lived in the same building, spoke the same language and were instilling in our children similar values but very different cautions.

From birth I had been taught to respect authority and accept the status quo. If I asked my father why, the answer was, "Because I said so." Fairness was defined by whoever had the clout. At the edge of adulthood, when my family feared I was becoming too critical of the world around me, my grandmother Lansburgh gave me a small bronze of the three monkeys: Hear-no-evil, See-no-evil, Speak-no-evil. Strange icons for a Jewish grandmother to be honoring in 1945. While the monkeys long since had lost their hold over me, the teachings of early childhood are hard to exorcise. I still believed the policeman was our friend, that good would triumph, and truth and justice prevail. I would have to learn a new set of commandments. "God Bless America" turned out to be a supplication, not an anthem.

A few years later Rob went off with a neighbor and her son to spend a day in New Jersey. Early afternoon, I got a call from the emergency room of a New Jersey hospital. Rob and his friend had been running through an empty lot when they were attacked by a German shepherd. The dog caught Rob by the leg and bit him squarely in the calf, extracting a chunk of skin and flesh from his calf. The dog's attack had been limited by the length of a steel chain and Rob had managed to pull himself away. But his leg was a mess and his troubles were not over. Unless we could establish that the dog was not rabid, he would need a series of painful injections in the stomach.

I called the local police precinct, presuming the dog had already been picked up and tested. But the sergeant was curiously laconic. I called the following day and the next, and finally called the office of the town's mayor. Still there was no response. Our pediatrician was becoming anxious. Time was running out and Rob woke up screaming in the middle of the night.

In frustration, I called my neighbor. Why had the police and the mayor done so little to help? "The police assume," she said, "that you are Black like us, that the boys were intruders on a white man's lot." I started to answer, then held my tongue.

That morning at work I wrote the mayor and police chief on CBS letterhead—*I've Got a Secret* was a CBS program—demanding an immediate response and sent the letter by registered mail. Within a day or so, I had my answer. The dog had been tested and showed no signs of rabies. "Not to worry, Mrs. Crichton," the police chief said. It was all there in black and white.

Among our neighbors at Morningside Gardens was Thurgood Marshall, then chief counsel for the NAACP Legal Defense Fund, his Hawaiian wife Cecilia and their two sons, John and Goody—Thurgood, Jr.—who was about the same age as Rob. Together the boys swapped Matchbox cars and watched cowboy movies with Goody's father, a large rumpled man who later drove our collective kids to school. I often saw Thurgood at the end of the day as he walked into the Gardens, loosening his tie, taking off his jacket, searching out the children.

With Thurgood, serious talk, political talk was out of bounds; he was under too much pressure as it was. In theory he'd destroyed the legal basis for segregation in America's public schools three years before when he had argued Brown vs. the Board of Education before the Supreme Court. But Southern schools were being integrated at the rate of only one per cent a year, and Thurgood and his colleagues were in the courts fighting the issue school by school, day after day.

In 1957 in Little Rock, Arkansas, nine Black children in starched white shirts and dresses tried to enter Central High while gun-toting members of the Arkansas National Guard jeered.

Though we were watching on a small black-and-white television set, the images were hot and immediate. We could see the faces of the children, their terror became ours, the South was no longer a distant country. The Governor declared that if any Black student put a foot inside the schoolhouse door, "blood would run in the streets."

Eisenhower wavered and only under pressure sent in the 101st Airborne. But the following fall, the violence continued, and the Governor, ostensibly to preserve law and order, closed down the school. Thurgood went back before the Supreme Court arguing that when banks were robbed, "you don't close the banks—you put the bank robbers in jail." The Justices found 9-0 in favor of Thurgood and the children.

While Martin Luther King, Jr. became a distant hero, Thurgood was our own. When he was appointed to the

U.S. Court of Appeals in 1961—a contentious appointment—Bob and I attended his swearing-in and then, after a few glasses of champagne, we went directly to the basement garage at La Salle Street where Bob and Judge Marshall affixed new license plates on Thurgood's Cadillac: license plates that read NYJ. Then Bob and Thurgood leaned against a steel upright, studied their handiwork, and began to laugh. History is often marked in small, curious, human-sized ways.

Our life seemed in balance in 1958. Sarah and Rob went to a nursery school in the Gardens, Jennifer stayed home with a wonderful sitter named Mattie, and there was a rhythm to our lives. On weekends Bob explored the neighborhood with the children. Just to the north of 125th Street he found a shop where live chickens were sold, the first live chickens our children had ever seen, and Bob entertained the storekeeper with his chicken raising talk.

Weekday mornings Bob and I would head out together for the D train at 125th Street and St. Nicholas Avenue. We'd cross a dreary playground at the edge of the projects, then turn down a narrow side street where out-of-work men passed their days on the stoops of run-down row houses. The post-war boom never reached Harlem. Bob made eye contact with everyone he passed, the litanies of *good mornings* were faithfully exchanged with men who held to their Southern ways.

Sarah and Jenny on the 80 La Salle Street terrace, with Rob looking on

Just before the subway stairs—the most crowded subway stop in Harlem—under a large American Airlines billboard that read "Get your tan in Miami," the neighborhood panhandler waited. Beggars made me anxious but Bob refused to quicken his gait. Sometimes he gave the fellow money, sometimes not; it was understood between them that it was always Bob's call.

One morning after a particularly generous contribution, we got down to the tollbooth only to discover Bob had given away all our money. Bob shrugged and bounded back up the stairs to ask the panhandler to lend us enough to get to work. That evening as we came up out of the station, the fellow was waiting. Standing in the center of a small group of men, he shouted, "There he is!" and pointed at Bob.

"I'll catch ya tomorrow," said Bob and kept right on walking. As we rounded the corner, we could still hear the men laughing.

CHAPTER 11

B y the end of 1958, Bob had finished *The Great Impostor*. The book was scheduled to come out in January 1959, and Random House was pleased. There was talk of a movie, an article for *Life*. Although it was all still just talk, I could see in Bob's walk, by the way he held his head, that he felt he'd turned a corner. "Don't look back," his father told him. *Argosy* offered him another job but Bob wrote the editor, "I still have to figure that as long as I can make it, I would most like to be a good writer."

Weeks before *The Great Impostor* was published, I ran into Herbie just outside his butcher shop on Broadway and 124th Street. Herbie and his brother Rudy were Jewish intellectuals who happened to be butchers like their father before them. Bob and I had run up a huge bill—over $200—and I was embarrassed and avoiding the shop. I explained to Herbie that we were waiting for some money to come in and—

Herbie interrupted me. He knew all about writers, he said, putting me at ease. His youngest brother was a writer, a Yale law professor and historian. In fact, there was a story about him that day on page seven in the *New York Times*. It sounds pat but it was true. We later learned that Herbie and Rudy had put their brother through college with the proceeds from the butcher shop. I followed Herbie into the shop where a large roasting chicken was cleaned, wrapped and added to our bill. The following Saturday, Bob went over to thank Herbie, and Herbie took him into the small room at the back where they sipped sherry and ate slices of salami.

During those weeks before *The Great Impostor* was published, Bob was clearing the decks: taking care of business, pawing the ground before starting another project. He wrote the manager of Morningside Gardens:

Mr. Arthur Frank
Morningside Gardens
80 LaSalle St.
New York 27

Dear Mr. Frank,

I want to take this chance to explain why,
especially this year, we have been frequently late
with rent payments. As I wrote a year ago, I am a
freelance writer and occasionally this almost
perforce produces a boom and bust economy. The

aim is to produce a big enough property so that you then have ample funds to ride over the bust periods without embarrassing yourself or others.

One other drawback is the rather haphazard manner of paying in the publishing field. I am at the moment owed some $4000 in magazine payments any or all of which could come tomorrow or two weeks from now. As an example, one of them is an article for LIFE on which I spent a month and which I have now been waiting 20 days to be paid for. (The article, incidentally, is scheduled to appear in the June 23 issue—although nothing is certain with LIFE until publication date—and is very funny, I insist).

In any event, the purpose of this letter is to tell you that I have finally latched on to a so-called big property. A book I have written has been purchased by Universal-International for a movie for a quite considerable sum of money. I have signed the contract and here again, exactly when and how I get paid I am not certain.

But what with the movie sale, the book sale, the paperback book sale, television and magazine rights, the corporation may rest assured that my immediate economic prospects are bright, even though at the specific moment you have had to alert the management to move its legal artillery into firing position. I also wanted to assure you that late payment of rent is not a chronic affliction but a temporary ailment that can quite soon be cured for what I hope is good.

Robert Crichton
Apt. 21F

When we left La Salle Street in the late 1960s, in spite of our inconstancy with the rent, Mr. Frank, the office manager, told Bob he hated to see us go. The Crichton papers, he said, were a La Salle Street treasure.

Bob wrote the same kind of personal letters to the IRS:

My book is now finished and I am once again doing magazine stories that bring in some form of regular income. I have enclosed a check for $50.00 for December and January payments and will be able to make a monthly payment.

I can't pay the full amount now since over the
year, I have run up a truly colossal stack of debts
but hope with this payment and a vow to continue
the next few months that the lien on my bank
account (there's only $33 in there) can be lifted if
only to spare the nuisance and embarrassment of
the affair. Would it be possible to do that, please?

At the beginning of 1959, the rhythm of our life was
thrown off once again. Bob wrote an ambivalent letter to
my Aunt Dorothy in advance of us seeing her and Dick
the following week:

I guess you are the person I should alert on this
delicate and touchy matter. I am trying to think of
some light way to broach the news but somehow
can't. It would seem that your niece is going to
have another baby.

Sometimes I think that we are the unwilling
victims of history. Here we are at a time of
explosive population growth and it would appear
that the thing is catching. With every sensible
precaution, somehow or other we have to add
another statistic. Please don't be too hard on poor
Judy. . .

And here we are practically grown out of our new house already.

When *The Great Impostor* was published, Random House took out an ad for six books: Faulkner's *The Mansion*, Robert Penn Warren's *The Cave*, James Michener's *Hawaii*, Moss Hart's *Act One*, Frank Sullivan's *A Moose in the Hoose* and Robert Crichton's *The Great Impostor*. We were stunned by the ad. The book did not deserve to be in the same sentence with Faulkner, Penn Warren, and Michener, and Bob knew it. But critics discovered what Bob's friends and family already knew. Bob was a superb storyteller. There were profiles of Bob in *The New York Post* and *The Newtown Bee*, articles and reviews in *Time* and *Newsweek*. When a woman columnist described Bob's wide mouth and clear blue eyes, I knew our life was changing.

With his writer friends, Bob was guarded. *The Great Impostor* was hack writing, he cautioned them. His father Kyle wrote that on the literary side he had some reservations about the book which he'd take up with Bob when the dust settled. But on the commercial side, he said, Bob had produced a triumph:

Not a triumph of art or even of story telling, but a
triumph of courage. I'd have given up halfway
through and I have a feeling that you were tempted
in that way more than once. In fact you hinted very
strongly to that effect, but I never took it seriously
at the time. Now I can see what you were talking
about. You had an impossible story to tell; you
were dealing with an impossible man . . .

I'm almost certain you'd have dropped it if you
hadn't felt a loyalty to us for backing you — and
the thing is a movie sale and probably a bestseller.
You'll write far better books in the future and not
have a touch of this luck. It's not enough, however,
to thank your lucky stars; give yourself credit for
having guts. When friends compliment you on
having written a great book, smile gratefully but
don't be taken in.

It's not a great book; it's something better: it's a
book that might have been written in the last half
hour by Davy Crockett at the Alamo.

Pop

Kyle was right. There were a dozen times Bob would have dropped the book but pride and loyalty kept him going. And the closest the book came to a bad review was a paragraph in *The Houston Chronicle* which declared Crichton should have visited Texas before he had the nerve to describe Huntsville as a town "30 miles north of Cut 'N Shoot out in what they call The Big Thicket, a rolling, sandy red-clay piney woods country that breeds mean, stringy cattle, men and razorback hogs." It was such a Bob Crichtonish sentence. I asked him if there really was a town called Cut 'N Shoot but never got an answer.

Yet for all the good reviews, *The Great Impostor* hovered in that limbo from which few books emerge, selling barely at all. We'd go into bookshops and it was clear the book was languishing, undisturbed on the shelves. If there were five copies in Scribner's on Monday, the same five were there on Tuesday. And we still hadn't settled our butcher bill.

Bob and I took our own steps to jolt the book out of limbo, and he and I began to plot our own promotion campaign. Within weeks we booked him on *The Mike Wallace Show, The Today Show, The Tonight Show, The Jack Paar Show.* The shows' bookers would interview Bob and, charmed by his stories, allot him five minutes. But Bob was a natural. Once on air, the spot would be extended. With Jack Paar, Bob cut loose and told a convoluted story about the first perfect martini ever made in East Glinty Glo, Pennsylvania; he was invited back before he left the stage. After Bob's second appearance on Jack Paar, sales of the book went from 41 copies a day to 1350, 1450, 1600. Every morning we would wait for the phone call with the latest sales figures.

There was a second printing, then a third. Then mid-August, the book made the *New York Times'* best-seller list and we all went to the Shanghai Cafe, a Chinese restaurant in the shadow of the elevated tracks on 125th Street and Broadway. We were on a roll.

The day *The Great Impostor* sold to the movies, Bob declared a holiday and Rob told a neighbor, "Poppa hit it rich in Hollywood and we're all going out to buy new shoes." Bob took us down to the midtown record store, Sam Goody's, where each of us selected an LP of our choice and then the five of us were off to see *The Pink Panther*. Big Bucks Bob, we called him, as we headed back to the Shanghai Cafe for the second time that month.

That very week, our old car up and died on our way home from Newtown. It was the same third-hand deathtrap Bob refused to feed oil that had coughed its way through our marriage. It began to splutter on the Merritt Parkway before it burst into flames. Bob led us up onto a knoll above the highway and as passersby watched, the five of us hooted and sang our damnable auto to its ashen grave. Bob called Kyle, who drove us back to New York. Even Kyle thought the timing was a miracle. The week we finally had money in our pockets, the old car up and died. Bob went out and bought another second-hand vehicle. But this one, he swore, was in pretty good condition.

With our new shoes and car, and cash in our pockets, we headed off to visit Bob's best friends from Harvard, Stuart and Barbara Bartle, who now lived in Charlottesville, where Stuart was the diagnostician on an open-heart surgery team. As we entered Charlottesville, Bob drove slowly down the main street until he found what he was searching for, what he knew he would find in the college town of the University of Virginia: J. Press. Bob had acquired his uniform at Harvard—khaki pants and sports coats—and it varied little over the years. In winter the khakis turned into corduroys but the philosophy remained the same. But it had been a long time since Bob last refreshed his wardrobe.

With J. Press in sight, when the traffic light turned red, Bob jumped out of the car, raced into J. Press and shouted at a stunned salesclerk, "Do you carry sports jackets 44 extra long?"

"Yes sir, one hundred dollars each."

"I'll take two," Bob said, forking over two $100 bills and taking the jackets straight from the hangers in the salesman's hands.

We laughed for years imagining how often the salesman must have entertained friends with the story of the customer who stopped at a red light, bought two jackets without trying them on, and leapt back into his car just as the light turned green.

We had a lovely spring weekend in Virginia and on the trip home Bob taught the children that spring travels north at fifteen miles a day. The blossoms were out when we left Charlottesville and by the time we got home to New York, the trees were just beginning to bloom.

The Great Impostor had sold to Hollywood for $64,000 but somehow Bob had managed to sign up with two agents. Each collected ten percent and twenty percent went to Random House. Bob repaid Kyle the $13,650 we had borrowed over the years. After taxes, we were left with less than a year's living money. Bob was back on Grub Street.

Later that spring, Jennifer was kidnapped.

Bob called me at the office, his voice flat, no embroidery. "Jennifer is gone," he said, "Call the police." A colleague gave me a shot of brandy, the smell made me ill, and I took a taxi home. I was seven months pregnant with Suzy and even the baby inside of me was quiet. For some hours, I had to remind myself to breathe.

Jennifer, our beautiful two-year-old Jennifer, had been in her stroller on the sidewalk just outside the door of the pharmacy where Mattie, our devoted sitter, had run in to pick up a prescription with the other two children. And when she returned, the stroller was empty.

I'd grown up with the story of the Lindbergh baby, with images of the anguished Lindberghs, the shroud over the small body, the manacled murderer seared on my mind. Neighbors had gathered outside our apartment and as I came down the hall from the elevator, I knew by their faces that Jenny was still missing.

In the living room, Bob and Mattie, Sarah and Rob waited, all but soundless. That morning our snail, one single aging monogamous snail, had astounded us with babies, scores of tiny babies not much larger than the head of a pin. It turns out snails are parthenogenic—they can reproduce without a partner. As the snails crawled out of their glass tank, Sarah returned them to the tank one at a time, grateful for the distraction.

Around five o'clock Bob was called to the local precinct to identify a child who turned out to be a four-year-old boy. The episode of false hope transformed our terror into fury. How could the police be so stupid? A neighbor

Mattie with Jenny

came in and gave Rob and Sarah supper. I could hear the clocks, though they were silent. Bob stood out on the terrace overlooking the city. The incinerator chimney directly above our apartment was belching smoke, engulfing Bob. But he never moved.

It was around dusk—seven o'clock, perhaps eight—when a young policeman arrived with Jenny on his shoulders, her face smudged with what remained of a candy bar he had given her as a treat. Sarah, a zealous older sister who had become Jen's other mother, mistook the chocolate for dried blood and burst into tears. Mattie, rocking in her chair, kept murmuring, "Thank you, Lord, thank you, Lord."

And I began to breathe for the first time in hours.

Bob collected Jen in his arms. She was confused but surprisingly calm. The cop had been walking his beat some fourteen blocks away, at Broadway and 111th Street, when he heard a screech of brakes and the uncontrolled screaming of a driver. He found Jenny sitting on the ground in front of the car, frightened but unharmed. We always supposed that whoever had taken Jenny—I always thought it must have been some unbalanced person who desperately wanted a baby of her own—thought the better of it, and released her in the middle of Broadway. We never knew what really had happened, and Jenny didn't have the words to tell us. That night, Bob and I took turns sleeping next to her, vigilant for signs of distress. But she slept through the night at peace in her own bed.[1]

---

[1] There was never any news coverage of this incident, no follow-up police report. The case seemed to end when Jenny was brought home.

CHAPTER 12

Susan Mary was born on August 28th, 1959, and nothing was ever the same after that. I knew something was wrong hours after her birth, the pretty limp baby with the large dark eyes who couldn't suck and was too weak to cry. Doctors offered hope she would catch on. I tried to believe them and suspected they were lying. My diary noted simply, "baby born." It was weeks before we gave Suzy a name. Euphoria had attended the birth of the first three children. Now Bob and I were filled with unspoken terror. We couldn't make eye contact. At night we slept with our backs to each other.

For weeks Suzy was kept alive by an eyedropper, fed at one-hour intervals twenty-four hours a day. Her lungs were not fully inflated, she could scarcely make a sound, her eyes never focused. There were times when she swung between life and death. No one knew what was wrong, and there were too many theories. Our family doctor urged us to let her go. We never spoke to him again. A fog of fatigue and sadness settled over the house. For a few months, a baby nurse and I spelled each other around the clock. Then the nurse was gone and I was on my own.

One morning when I was dressing the baby, Rob ran into the room, a cowboy hat on his head, a holster around his waist, and shot off his cap gun. Startled, Suzy was frozen with fear, her great brown eyes terrified. But she was soundless, always soundless, not able to cry or call out. I screamed at Rob and then wanted to hug him but couldn't leave Suzy. And there was a wall now between me and Bob. Our intimacy was shattered, our parenting split in two. Weekends he took over the older three children, and I stayed home with Suzy. Too often at night we fought over details not worth the fighting and fell asleep in isolation.

On our first family outing with Suzy, the six of us set out for the Central Park Zoo. The older children wore matching plaid coats with velvet collars we had bought at an outlet shop in Brooklyn. Sarah was five, Rob three, Jenny two. For the moment I tried to repress my sadness. As Bob played with the older children, I sat on a bench near the Alice in Wonderland statue as Suzy slept in her pram. Across the way, I saw a gray, sad-faced mother with a retarded daughter about twelve years old. I could see directly into the heart of their life, the love and the pain, the embarrassment that wasn't supposed to be there, and grasped the endless, exhausting patience their life required, that my life would require. While Bob helped our children climb the bronze statue of Alice, I began to retreat beyond my family's reach.

Together Bob and I went on endless doctor visits, held long talks with specialists who had no answers. It was a year before Suzy's muscles acquired enough tension to allow her to sit up, and it was over three years before she began to walk. On the long drives to Newtown to visit Kyle and May, she would stare out the window with unseeing eyes. The first time she responded to the lights on the George Washington Bridge as we drove back home, I began to cry and Bob led the older children in a rousing rendition of The George Washington Bridge song. "George Washington Bridge, oh the Geor-or-ge Washington Bridge! . . ."

Sometime in 1960 Bob wrote our friends the Bartles:

Judy has gone back to work for a month and a half
on *I've Got A Secret*. In a terrible sequence of
events we both made an error of $3,980 in our
bank account and the federal tax people demand
$4,500 more in taxes. As of yesterday I am at once
$8,000.00 poorer than I ever knew and now panic
begins to mount once again. This was the whole
safety edge and now I am back on Grub Street with
a rush and a thud. Unbelievably depressing. It's ok

to get in a hole if you have a steady income but I have not one cent at the moment coming in. Only deeper and deeper in I go. Do you know of a little piney goober farm somewhere a few miles out of town along the river?

No news, really. Children all fine. Susan coming along, coming along. Sarah can read anything you can . . .

The letters about Suzy are mixed in with letters about *The Great Impostor*. She was born just months after the book was published. Bob tried to infuse our lives with a sense of optimism that I couldn't share. *The Great Impostor* was still on the *Times* bestseller list and Dorothy sent Bob a copy of a double-acrostic that incorporated a quote from his book.

Of all things that have happened, nothing seems to have quite so impressed people as having my sacred prose reproduced for the double-acrostic. That really finally proves to everyone that the book has merit. That makes it official. Reviews be damned—the Saturday Review has officially put the seal of approval on the prose.

The letter went on, as all his letters did at the time, to talk about the baby.

> Susan, the new one, you know, seems to be holding her own. It would now appear beyond any doubt to be a case of myasthenia gravis. That is a hell of a thing to have to cheer about but we are cheering since every other prognosis was unbelievably worse. As long as we control her medicine, there is every chance that she will be absolutely normal.

Too much happened in the next year or so for continuity of memory. Bob seemed collected but I was in suspension, angry that he could not share my terror of the future. I would goad, he would resist: "I don't think there's anything more to say." The outside world slid in and out of focus. Kyle and May were unbearably sad but loving and attentive. I wanted to know more about Billy and how whatever affected him might relate to Suzy, but I couldn't bring myself to ask.

My own family was embarrassed. My mother, who now lived in the Virgin Islands, would come to New York on occasion. But she never came to see Suzy, having locked her in a psychic closet. There was no room in my mother's heart for imperfect children.

I began an endless dance with doctors trying to discover what was wrong with our slow child who was pudgy and pretty, with rich chestnut hair, enormous brown eyes and a snub nose like a baby doll's, but gently nonresponsive. Much of what they said was nonsense and very expensive. She may catch up, she has a displaced hip, we don't know the answers but her reflexes are slow. Suzy loved the attention as we moved from one doctor's office to the next. But on too many days, I wished us both dead and then loathed myself for those feelings. I could never seem to escape from my own anger.

We were sent to see a tiny pediatrician, a lovely birdlike man named Dr. Bass who had been a pediatrician for almost 60 years. Everything about him had dried up except his head and hands. He took Suzy in his arms, explored her body limb by limb with such gentleness she never knew she was being examined. "This is terrible," he said as his hands kept traveling, "The child has no muscle tone. I'm so sorry." He handed her back to me.

Everything was puzzling about Suzy's condition. There was no explanation for the laxness of her muscles or her difficulty sucking. Yes, her development was slow. Yes, she was retarded. But what did that mean? We told him that when we went into the room that Suzy shared with Sarah in the morning, Bob and I could see the

*A three-year-old Suzy gazing at Stuart Bartle as
he played harmonica on Cape Cod*

intelligence in her eyes. Dr. Bass said that he believed he could find the answer. Curiously I believed him. In fact, I had no choice.

Some days later he called to say that he'd been reading and thought he'd found a lead. The following day,

Dr. Bass took us to see a large overweight messy specialist in an East Side office with an overcrowded waiting room. Dr. Kermit Osserman smoked cigars while his stomach pushed against his untidy desk.

Osserman placed Suzy on the examining table.

"Aaah," he said, poking her with a hook. "Aaah." He prodded her until she cried.

"That's enough, doctor," Dr. Bass said sternly.

Osserman blinked and ended his experiment. Returning to his desk, retrieving his cigar, he agreed with the suspicion that Suzy had a rare case of juvenile myasthenia gravis, a neuromuscular disease. He injected our baby with medication. Within seconds, she was kicking her flaccid legs and screaming with a strength we had never heard. Bass looked concerned, Osserman was reassuring. "We have," he said, "a confirmed diagnosis."

For the next six or seven years, that's what we told the world: Suzy has a rare neuromuscular disease. Myasthenia gravis. She may be mildly retarded as well but the underlying problem is myasthenia gravis.

It was a comforting diagnosis, dealing with a problem of chemistry and not the brain. How important that seemed to be. Around my house when I was growing up, the worst epithet ever heard was, "he's a congenital idiot." And now I had given birth to a — I wished I could pray but I had no faith to fall back on.

Suzy was given a medication called neostigmine, a cousin to curare, measured in drops because even the smallest overdose might kill her. Three times a day, we went through the ceremony of measuring the medicine, then watching the brightening in her eyes, the tension in her legs build. Bob and I became convinced the medication worked—perhaps only modestly, but no matter. He wrote my sister, his sister and my father variations on the letter below:

There is no word on the baby. Myasthenia gravis is simply a very serious disease. It can at times be terrible and at times be quite mild. As of now, Susan is way behind. This does not mean she is a retarded child. When she gets her tension, she is normal, but at several times during the day, the balance of chemicals in her body is not exactly right. She is flaccid and unable to help herself. At other times the least exertion exhausts her so much that although she is as hungry as any baby and wants food terribly, she can't cry out for it and she can't even swallow. She can taste it and can't get it. As the doctors admit, this is bound to have some tough psychological eventualities.

I am trying to write ten letters. Everyone is mad at us and I have to tell full details of Susan. We will try to keep you informed but for a month or two things will be pretty tight around here.

Dr. Osserman insisted on checking Suzy regularly and he made it known he preferred to be paid in cash. Long after I stopped believing, I believed. There was no alternative. Gentle, reassuring Dr. Bass had died, and no one else offered even tenuous hope.

The summer of 1960, we drove to Cape Cod to a rough old clapboard house, the last and largest in a line of seven cottages on a steep dune overlooking Cape Cod Bay. On the side of Corn Hill that ran alongside the Pamet River, Bob and the children collected cat-tails and looked for beavers that didn't exist. Outside the backdoor, a great flat of sand extended for yards and became the field for running bases. Stuart and Barbara Bartle, their four children and their orange cat named Willoughby took the cottage next door, and Bob ran summer camp for our collective children. I had found Corn Hill by calling the Truro telephone operator and asking her to recommend a nice place for a family with a passel of kids and little money. And here we were.

We had retreated for a month with three crates of books. Each child borrowed ten volumes from the public library on 125th Street, the special summer borrowing allowance in those more trusting days. There was no phone on Corn Hill, no radio, no television. I didn't drive and life was bordered by the weather, the children and the sea. Bob wallowed in the privilege of summer read-aloud every evening and invented spooky ghost stories for the children as I tried to restore the inner balance I had lost.

The first year of Suzy's life, when I had stayed home to care for her, had been one of the loneliest I'd ever known. The first months I'd been fearful she would die, then fearful that she wouldn't. I was estranged from my husband, estranged from my children, estranged from myself drowning in my evil thoughts.

With Suzy and Jen on the Corn Hill beach

Corn Hill became a closed circle. Our life was tied to the hill, beyond the reach of the outside world, the six of us together. By the third week, when we were running low on money, Bob and the children took their pails down to the cove where the mussels lived. Every leftover in the refrigerator was put to use and when Bob used the car—and he was using it less and less—he coasted down the hills to save on gas. "Field expediency," he called it.

One extraordinary morning while Suzy was being cared for by a blond angel of a mother's helper and Bob was off with the older children on a nature walk, I sat by myself at the edge of the bluff and studied an ant's convoluted journey between a decaying piece of sandwich and an anthill in the grass. Over several hours as the ant renewed its larder, I began to renew my soul. It was the first empty morning I had had in years. That night, Bob and I talked, really talked, for the first time since Suzy was born. Or at least we tried.

We had long abandoned Bob's great book course, our evenings too ragged for the classics. I read few books at all anymore, and the newspaper was scanned—or not—on the subway in the morning. But in the peace of that summer for the first time in years, I had stretches of time, sometimes hours of time, and I began to read again. In a small generous book by Anne Morrow Lindbergh, *Gift from the Sea,* I saw a reflection of myself. Lindbergh had five children and a prominent, dominant and creative husband. Her love for them all was beyond question. But she had come to see herself as a trapeze artist, trying to balance all the demands in her life. In the opening pages of the book, she wrote:

> The shape of my life today starts with a family. I have a husband, five children and a home . . . I have also a craft, writing, and therefore work I want to pursue. The shape of my life is, of course, determined by many other things; my background and childhood, my mind and its education, my conscience and its pressures, my heart and its desires. I want to give and take from my children and husband, to share with friends and community, to carry out my obligations to man and to the world, as a woman, as an artist as a citizen.

> But I want first of all—in fact as an end to these other desires—to be at peace with myself.

I felt Lindbergh was talking directly to me. She wrote of the *caravan of complications* in her life, of making ends meet in a thousand ways, of providing spiritual and educational guidance for her children and then having nothing left for herself. From the cadence of her sentences, I knew that she had lost her breath as I had lost mine. She catalogued the essential demands for which she was responsible:

Food and shelter, meals. planning, marketing, bills, doctors, dentists, appointments, medicine, school conferences, clothes, shopping, letting skirts down and sewing buttons on, or finding someone else to do it. It involves friends, my husband's, my children's, my own.

What a circus act we women perform every day of our lives. It puts the trapeze artist to shame. Look at us. We run a tight rope daily, balancing a pile of books on the head. Baby carriage, parasol, kitchen chair, still under control. Steady now!

The book was a meditation on finding peace, remaining whole in the midst of an over-demanding life. Alone at the beach for two weeks, Lindbergh wrote of shedding not only her clothes but her vanity.

Vanity. I skidded to a stop over the word. How entangled I was by vanity, consumed by vanity. Vanity contributed to my fury over Suzy. I had moved into marriage and then into motherhood dragging with me all my childhood insecurities. My sense of self had been defined first by my husband, my brilliant handsome husband, and then by my children—my bright, smart, engaging children. I had enjoyed the compliments of friends, the looks of strangers, the recognition that we were an uncommon tribe.

And then came Suzy. I was embarrassed by Suzy, my passive child with the wandering eye and the odd look on her face. Before Suzy, I thought I lived in a world of unconditional love. In fact, I offered love to my husband and children in return for their shoring up my ego. It was neither fair nor realistic. Suzy had lost before she had begun, and I had, too. Now, with the gift of time, I began to re-examine my relationships with Bob and the children, including Suzy. Particularly Suzy.

It was on the Cape that Bob taught himself to swim, how to really swim. He was afraid of the water, but more afraid of being helpless if one of the children got in trouble. Every morning, down in the shallows, he swam parallel to the shore, practicing the crawl and the butterfly stroke. He understood the butterfly was not much good for lifesaving. With every stroke, he swept up a confusion of water. But it was a wonderfully showy way to swim.

After breakfast, Bob and Stuart took their positions for running bases, a simple-minded game the children never seemed to tire of. While the kids raced between two bases thirty feet apart, Bob and Stuart tossed a softball back and forth, ostensibly trying to tag them out. There was a muddled kind of scoring only Bob understood. At a certain point in every game, the men would begin to throw the ball harder and faster, forgetting the children and challenging each other.

Bob would catch the ball behind his back inches off the sand, dive for the ball, leap for the ball. He had the look of a ballplayer, the rangy body and long strong fingers of a ballplayer, and the absolute conviction that if he only wanted it hard enough, he could still make the major leagues. Stuart said Bob could never be a ballplayer because he threw left-handed and batted right. Bob paid no attention. Well into his forties, he was still practicing his swing and tracking every professional player older than he.

They were an odd pair, those two, with a marvelous ability to be goofy with each other. Years later, when the twelve of us, the Bartles and the Crichtons, went to see *The Planet of the Apes*, Bob and Stuart left the movie theater racing down the sidewalk, knees bent, shrieking and scratching, with the children right behind them, mimicking their fathers who were mimicking the apes as Barbara screamed after them, "Boys! Boys!"

Best friends since freshman year at Harvard, both were sports fanatics, both drank martinis and, most important to Bob at the time, both had been infantrymen. Stuart had also suffered through the freezing

Bob and Stuart Bartle inexpertly sawing a log on Corn Hill

miserable Christmas of 1944 in combat and although he always referred to his own combat experiences as minuscule, he had seen enough.

On the surface, Bob and Stuart seemed mismatched. Stuart had been pre-med, studying physics and chemistry. To please Bob, he began reading Proust but never got much beyond the first fifty pages. He was escaping the WASP enclaves of his childhood and Bob was determined to rescue him from the predictable and boring. They hung out together in tough Boston bars and together founded the Student Apathy League but were far too apathetic to recruit other members, or so the story, so the joke of it, went.

Tall, blond and delicate in manner, Stuart was tougher than he appeared. When we met, he was selling blood and swatches of skin from his inner arms to help pay his tuition for medical school. By the late 1950s, he was working with the open-heart surgery team at the University of Virginia, and Barbara—Barbara Bishop Bartle who wore black strapless bathing suits and a large straw hat to protect her blond hair and pale skin—was a civil rights activist engaged in lunchroom sit-ins. The Bartles were central to Bob's life and, in time, to mine.[2]

In the closing days of our vacation, I was home alone with Suzy when a Western Union messenger drove up the steep winding hill with a telegram for Robert Crichton. In 1960 telegrams still had weight: We regret to inform you —Fill in the blank with your son, your father, your brother. Why did I always envision the darkest option? Telegrams could also herald the birth of a baby, a wedding, a party.

This telegram was none of the above. Robert Kennedy was asking Bob to join his brother's presidential campaign staff. Bob and Robert Kennedy had been friends at the Benedictine boarding school, Portsmouth Priory. Both Bob and Bobby had loved the Priory with its mix of the religious, the idealistic and the intellectual, and at

---

[2]It was Stuart who became a medical detective when Bob crossed the line of reason, and Stuart and Barbara who helped save my sanity when I began to understand that Bob was losing his.

Portsmouth, both had been able to shake free of the forces holding them down at home. Kennedy was beyond his father's immediate reach; Old Joe was a tyrant. And Bob, who had been a captive of the jocks in Bronxville, was freed to acknowledge his love of books.

In their senior year, Bobby was sent off to a socially prominent prep school, but after the War, the two resumed their friendship at Harvard. The telegram from Bobby Kennedy was one of those serendipitous happenings that often seemed to mark our life. The Kennedy brothers, with their extraordinary reach, had found Bob on our hilltop, and were waving money and the promise of things to come.

Bob and I had worked briefly in both of Adlai Stevenson's presidential campaigns, first as volunteers in 1952, then as paid staffers in 1956. I'd worked in the speakers' bureau, and Bob had been one of a cadre of writers turning out material to use in speeches. Stevenson wrote his own speeches but those who spoke for him often needed help.

There was a personal quality to campaigns in those days. The staffs were relatively small, and Bob and I met Stevenson several times, felt his wit and decency, and grieved when he lost. Stevenson was an unlikely looking candidate: bald, with the baggy eyes of a student who'd been up all night. He refused to be swept up by anti-communist hysteria and talked of the need to protect America from her overzealous friends. "To strike freedom of the mind with the fist of patriotism is an old and ugly subtlety," he said. Arguing against the arms race, Stevenson said, "At the end of this road lies bankruptcy or world catastrophe." The fear of an atomic war was always at the edge of our thinking.

It was stunning to have an almost-friend run for the presidency. So when the telegram arrived from Bobby Kennedy, I was excited by the promise of another campaign. Bob was less certain. He wanted to go back to his writing. The telegram lay unanswered on the kitchen counter as Bob took long walks down the beach to mull it over. He disliked Bobby's Cold War rhetoric and his connections to McCarthy, and he thought Jack was a lightweight playboy. A week after the telegram arrived, Bob went down to the telephone booth at the base of Corn Hill and called Kennedy to turn him down.

On the day before we headed back to New York, sitting on the sand and holding Suzy between us, I asked Bob again about his brother Billy. He had no answers. All he could remember was that Billy had an uncontrollable temper. Suzy was still the gentlest of children. We had yet to see her angry except for those occasions when we tried to curb her appetite for cookies.

When Suzy was first born, I took a vow to become the best of all mothers to a handicapped child. I would succeed where others had failed. It was a vow taken for all the wrong reasons, for ego-driven reasons. That summer on the Cape, I found enough peace to let go of anger. But I had yet to make room for my youngest child. I held her, I kissed her, and I tried to smile. But it never occurred to me that in time, I would fall in love with Suzy without forcing it, just as I had done with the others.

CHAPTER 14

The Rascal and the Road, Bob's follow-up to *The Great Impostor,* was a book he should never have written. The account of his journey with Fred Demara was conceived in the confusion following Suzy's birth and written in haste. It was a terrible time and Bob was far more troubled than I understood. Any pretense of ambition was buried by the darkness of our moods and an ever-growing pile of medical bills. We took an oath that Bob would never write another book just to make money again.

Around the same time, Kyle was writing a memoir, carefully censoring almost everything that mattered. *Total Recoil* came out to a few mildly favorable reviews by friends and virtually no sales. *Rascal* fared no better. In his notebook, Bob wrote about himself and his father, "There is a decided trait of dishonesty in our personal writing, a protecting of ourselves that is fatal." *Total Recoil* was a collection of disconnected anecdotes about a life left unexamined in that book. When Bob wrote *The Rascal and the Road,* he too was writing in disguise.

When D.H. Lawrence critiqued Kyle's writing in a letter he wrote to Kyle in 1925, he warned that "where the living feeling should be, it's blank: blank." It was a cruel assessment and an accurate one. Kyle was too guarded, too much the Scotsman to risk revelation in a novel or, forty years later, a personal memoir.

The best thing about Bob's book was the dedication:

> For My Father
> He despaired of the project from the start. He was
> convinced the journey out on the road was
> inspired by idiocy and tainted with some madness.
> But it was Kyle who, when the whole project was
> on the tilting edge of disaster, salvaged it all by his
> real encouragement and his real money, neither of
> which he was ever prone to squander.

Now Kyle had died.

Bob and Kyle had become particularly close in the months before his death. One crazy evening in early fall, Kyle arrived at our apartment unexpectedly, in his porkpie hat, with a cigar clenched between his teeth, his one good lung wheezing, to deliver hand-me-down children's furniture that May had collected for Suzy. Kyle had parked his car on 127th Street and asked a group of boys standing on the corner if they would help an old man lug his goods to La Salle Street. And so they had. A high chair was carried on the back of a young teenager, a playpen in the hands of another. Several other boys stood out in the hall, along for the ride. When I opened our door, the group of Black youngsters smiled, and Kyle teased them and clapped them on the back. Kyle—and Bob, too—moved through life on the assumption that the world would meet him on his own terms. More often than not, it seemed to.

Kyle must have had an intimation that he didn't have long. Around the time of that surprise visit, he told Bob, "When I go, May will insist I found God. Don't argue." Then he was dead and May indeed said that Kyle had died a religious man. There was a wake at the house in Newtown and later at the funeral parlor, where cousins, uncles, brothers, friends, writers and leftists tried to talk Kyle back to life. But his crossword puzzle was unfinished, his hat sat on the bookcase and, no matter how he tried, Bob could not take his place.

Driving back to the city the night after Kyle's funeral, on a trip Bob had driven hundreds of times, Bob made a wrong turn, and at two in the morning in the dead dark streets of the Bronx, we were hopelessly lost, and Bob began to cry.

Kyle's death was much like my grandfather's; only in retrospect could one discern the warnings. Two charming

Kyle in the living room in Newtown;
he was 64 when he died

men seemingly in command of their lives at one moment, and at the next, dying suddenly, surrounded by strangers. Kyle collapsed outside his favorite coffee shop on the corner of 44th Street and Sixth Avenue. My grandfather Percy Lansburgh died in the lobby of the Savoy-Plaza.

As a child I had spent days trying to find a metaphysical trick that would allow me to reach out and say a proper goodbye to my grandfather. When I failed, I settled on trying to preserve the sound of his voice, the look on his face, the feel of my hand in his. Every night before I went to sleep, I would pull memories from the recesses of my brain, teasing out the details so that I would never forget them. I would now try to do the same with Kyle.

After Kyle died, with the help of his papers and his fragmented memoir, I tried to deconstruct the myths surrounding his life. The real Kyle had been hidden beneath a clutter of affectations and a mountain of anecdotes. The anecdotes were entertaining, to be sure, but Kyle existed in the silences between and beneath his words. He used the word *fathead* the way other men used *darling*. All his grandchildren understood that. When Kyle batted a child on the head with a newspaper, the child would feel loved and climb up on his lap. He had made me feel loved as well. Where my parents failed, when Bob wandered, when I lost my way—Kyle was always there.

Bob had taken an office in a midtown hotel, favored by transients and German flight crews and couples stealing two-hour retreats. In the months following Kyle's death, Bob was caught up in an interior existence about which I knew little. The best writing he did during that time were delicate sketches he wrote for his own amusement which no one ever saw:

A superb example of the flash of the absurd.

I arrive at work to find that the little cigar stand in the hotel is closed. I don't ask about it but a man gets on the elevator with me and he asks.

He's dead, the operator says.

But he was here only Friday. I talked to him here this Friday.

He's dead. He died.

The man looks out of the door at the little shuttered shop. This was the end. This was what he did all of his days.

He was here so many days, the man said.

No one answers him. And suddenly he turns to me and just as suddenly we both smile, a wide, open-eyed deep into the eyes smile.

We had both just seen the absurd and we knew it in each other.

There was nothing to do but first smile and then laugh because men always laugh when they recognize the truth.

Bob began some odd and interesting projects: a play, a movie, a television documentary, an essay on J. D. Salinger. But Sarah and Rob now went to private school, and Jen would soon follow, and even with the scholarships that covered the bulk of the tuition, the amount we were expected to produce was daunting. Faced with the daily dollar drain, there was not the time for serious work. Bob took odd jobs for hire, wrote the narration for industrial films, worked for Allen Funt on the television show *Candid Camera* (Funt was a tough man, but he paid well). But every job Bob took seemed to carry him further from the work he cared about. As Bob wrote later in an essay,

> The only thing I ever wanted to accomplish in my life was to write a good novel. I wanted this so much that I came to think of myself as being a novelist even though I had never written one. Despite this little failing I was quite convinced that were I to die right then, my obituary would read Crichton, Novelist, Writes Last Chapter because everyone would know how much it meant to me.

And it would be only fair; I had all the novels in my head. All that was lacking was the technical formality of transferring them to paper.

This state of affairs went on until I was past thirty. When no novel appeared, in order to account for the void and save my self-respect, I was driven to conclude that I was a classic example of the pitfalls of Grub Street. I was a freelance magazine writer then, living from one assignment to the next, always one advance behind, and I saw myself as a victim of the literary sharecropper system, as hopelessly snared in my web of circumstance as those wretched cotton farmers James Agee described in *Let Us Now Praise Famous Men*.

There were times when he found ways to get off the plantation. One night, in the midst of the pre-supper madness as the children marched around the living room, singing "Food Glorious Food!", Bob peeled off into the kitchen to tell me that *Argosy* magazine was sending him to Paris to help judge the most beautiful girl in the world contest.

"You're going to Paris to find the most beautiful girl in the world?" I was in a fury. I was tired of being broke, tired of Bob's flirtations, tired of being practical and strong, and too proud to tell anyone about the rotter I had married.

While Bob was away in France, Sarah and I made a papier-mâché mask of Templeton the Rat from E. B. White's *Charlotte's Web*. Templeton was, I think, my finest act of sublimation.

The day Bob was due back, Sarah and Rob drew "Welcome Home Daddy" signs, we all blew up balloons, the front door was decorated, and I very much wanted to see him. But Bob never showed up. He called from a noisy bar in Germany where he had just bet a newly-acquired friend that he was married to the most under-standing of women.

Wrong.

During the trans-Atlantic call we couldn't afford, he explained that after the contest, instead of hanging around Paris, he had rented a car and driven east, alone, back to the battlefields he'd never forgotten. When he crossed into Germany, a border guard commanded "Achtung!" and triggered memories Bob had long been repressing.

I heard every word Bob said and did not believe a word.

The first evening Bob was back from Europe, he rid the house once and for all of Jenny's imaginary, trouble-making wolf. For months the wolf had been Jenny's constant and friendly companion. She would talk to the wolf, pet the wolf, play with the wolf. But without explanation, the wolf turned and became threatening, and Jenny would run from her bed with terrified screams. Now with Bob back from Europe, just as Jenny was about to slide into sleep, she flew from her room with a blood-curdling scream. The wolf would have to go.

Bob ran into the room she shared with Rob, grabbed the animal from the lower bunk of the bunk bed, and marched out of the apartment with Jenny at his heels. As he wrangled the imaginary creature struggling in his arms, he opened the incinerator hatch and shoved the wicked wolf down down down into its deepest recesses. Then, singing *Ding dong the wolf is dead,* he led a peaceful Jenny back to bed.

It might have been wiser to help a four-year-old untangle fantasy from reality but that did not occur to either of us. Bob had a way of dealing with demons, all except his own.

There were times when Bob was an inconstant husband and I often wasn't sure about my suspicions. But after ten years of marriage, he could still walk in the door and pull me back from the precipice.

When I wasn't suspicious or exhausted—four kids and a full-time job was a lot—he was still the most interesting man I'd ever met.

In the meadow on the hill overlooking the Newtown house, we were lying in the tall grass which had yet to be mowed. It had been too long since we'd been alone on that hill, too long since we'd been alone. At the edge of the meadow was an asparagus patch gone wild and rows of apple trees planted long before by someone we never knew. Down below the trees, the lilacs were in bloom.

"Isn't this enough?" Bob asked.

We could hear the children laughing in the field next to the house, and he didn't need an answer.

When we had arrived the night before, armsful of lilacs had been placed in a large Lalique vase on a round table at the far end of the living room. As long as I'd been coming to Newtown, spring had been marked by a lilac display. The vase was very heavy and it used to take all of Kyle's strength to carry it from the cupboard in the kitchen to that table, with May saying "Careful, careful" and Bob saying "Let me do it, Pop," and Kyle bellowing "I can do it just fine" as he hobbled into the living room.

Now Kyle was gone but the Lalique vase was full of flowers.

May was pleased when we asked her how she had managed without Kyle. "I have my ways," she said. She would rarely admit that life was harder now. Using a step stool, she had taken the vase down from the cupboard, placed it in a roasting pan, tied a string to the roasting pan handle, and pulled it through the house to the table by the window. Once the vase was in place, she dragged in pots of water from the kitchen and filled the vase cup by cup. Only then had May taken her knife and gone up into the fields to cut the lilacs.

Newtown had its traditions.

Near the barn was a small, charmless house that had never quite been finished. Kyle always intended to rent it out in exchange for some help around the place. Instead it became a shelter for those down on their luck. For a time, the house was taken over by a writer named Bill Courtney, his wife and five children, and their old, ailing horse. At first we were pleased to have the horse; it seemed to legitimize calling the place a farm. But Bob paid more attention to Courtney's horse than Courtney did. When Bob was growing up in Albuquerque, herds of wild horses still galloped across the mesa and that led him to believe he knew about horses. He did not. But he brushed the animal, fed him and, putting a blanket on the horse's curving back, lifted the children up to take a ride, sometimes two at a time. When the horse became too ill to reach the oats in the trough, Bob fed him by hand.

Caring for the horse was an act of mercy that almost killed Bob. He was allergic to animals, to dust and pollen, to my lipstick and scores of substances we had yet to pinpoint. While caring for the horse, he once sneezed to the point where I feared he'd have a stroke. His eyes ran, his skin turned blotchy. But Bob was haunted by that horse. One winter evening he came down from the barn to say the horse was dying. He took an old blanket from the attic and sat in the barn with the horse's head in his lap and kept him company until the end.

In the meadow, when Bob had said "Isn't this enough?", I knew it was a gentle reproach of sorts. He wanted us to build a life in which the children found joy, free from dependence on elaborate entertainment. In the fall, he would spend hours raking, building a giant pile of leaves at the base of the stone wall in front of the house, and the children would fly off the wall, sink into the leaves, almost drown in the leaves. And after every jump, Bob would pile them up again.

He feared that in New York the children would be smothered by the materialism crowding in around them. They needed blank paper to write and to draw, and empty time to think, and balls and bats and books and generosity of spirit, and very little more. He would teach them all to stretch their minds and legs. Every walk would become an adventure. On a dirt road, miles beyond the farm, there was a house where an entire family had escaped a fire by jumping out a window. Bob and the children stood in front of the house and contemplated the experience: the smoke and the flames, and then the triumph of survival.

Bob wearing his Scottish tam, with Sarah,
Jenny and Rob near the barns in Newtown

There were times Bob went too far and asked too much of the children. On an icy February day with a cruel wind blowing, he walked Sarah, Rob and Jen across the narrow footpath on the George Washington Bridge. When the going gets tough, he'd say, the tough get going. But with the wind lashing ice onto their faces, it was a harrowing crossing. By the time they reached New Jersey, the children were all but paralyzed by the cold. Bob had to carry Jenny, and he no longer had any feeling left in his own feet which had never fully recovered from the frostbite he suffered in the War.

There on the Palisades side of the bridge, with ice clinging to their jackets, looking like a tableau composed by Charles Dickens, Bob, with no money in his pockets, flagged down a Greyhound bus coming in from Chicago. The driver mercifully stopped and carried them to within a block of our door.

As they stumbled into the apartment, Sarah stilled my fury. "We had a great adventure, Mom!" she said.

Sarah knew and I knew that her father was the only man alive who would have the wit, the gall, to hail a Greyhound bus on the George Washington Bridge as if it were a taxi.

Jenny, Sarah, Suzy, Bob and Rob
in the La Salle Street living room

In the photograph of Bob and the children, Suzy looks straight into the camera, her wide eyes made wider by her medication. Sarah and Jenny are laughing on the couch, teeth missing, joy in their faces. Robby stands next to Bob, his smile only slightly more muted. And Bob is smiling, too. The cameraman has put them all at ease except for Suzy who seems to struggle to understand the moment.

How to explain Suzy. I never found it easy. But by the time that she was two, I knew that Bob was right. There was an interesting person emerging from this quiet child. She was the most sociable person, passing from one set of arms to another, never having to compete for love. Her survival required that someone always be in attendance, and someone always was. Suzy choked easily, and we learned to put our fingers down her throat to relieve the blockage; Dr. Heimlich had yet to invent his maneuver. The choking incidents must have been as terrifying for Suzy as they were for us, but she was not an anxious child. At three she'd never known anger, never been scolded. *No* was a word reserved for others. She was too sedentary to ever get into trouble. She never had to be pulled away from a curb or restrained from an electrical outlet.

But now she was beginning to walk. Suzy made her way into Rob and Jen's room and knocked down Rob's elaborate city he'd spent hours constructing out of blocks. Caught by surprise, Rob simply said, "Oh Suzy" and rebuilt his city. Some hours later, Suzy followed me into the kitchen and, quick as a whippet, reached up and turned on the gas on the stove. I was astounded. "No, Suzy, no!" I said, picking her up and carrying her back into the living room.

A few minutes later, Suzy was in the kitchen again, laughing. This time the flames leapt higher and her face had a devilish expression I had never seen before. A third time, and a dishrag caught fire. I was angry, frightened, furious with myself. I threw the rag into the sink. The flames had yet to die as I picked up Suzy and, shouting, "No, no, no!", slapped her on the hand.

The slap was meant to be symbolic but it carried greater weight than I intended. At this first sign of my anger, Suzy retreated into some distant mode of consciousness beyond my reach. Her eyes were open but she would not engage. For hours I begged her to come back, but she gave no response.

I knew a family with an autistic child and now I feared for Suzy. In the early 1960s, it was believed that autism was a psychiatric disturbance triggered by a cold, unloving parent—usually a cold, unloving mother, "the refrigerator mother." It was one of the cruelest errors in psychiatric history, condemning thousands of parents—mostly mothers—for crimes they had not committed.

The theory has long since been discredited. But at the time I believed my lapse into frustration and anger had driven Suzy crazy. I was drowning in guilt. Every evil thought I'd had since the day she was born replayed in my brain. Perhaps Suzy had intuited all my old rotten feelings, absorbed them and withdrawn from a mother who did not know how to love her.

Come back, Suzy, wherever you are. We all said it, we all thought it. Bob tried to reach her, Sarah too. But Suzy did not return until the following day. When she finally surfaced, she clung to me and I to her. I'm not sure which of us was more relieved. There was so much about Suzy I would have to learn and so much that I would have to teach her, beginning with the fact that anger is not death, that *no* is a part of life, that even the most beloved and loving can have rotten thoughts—and move on.

It was not the last time that Suzy retreated. Her nervous system had its limits. As she grew up and moved into a less cloistered life, when too many stimulants crowded in on her, she would twiddle and play with her fingers before her eyes. Her eyes would cross and she would disappear into herself, often with a slight bemused smile. The deeper she went, the faster her fingers moved. But we could usually retrieve her with a gentle touch or a quiet "Come back, Suzy, wherever you are." And Suzy would resurface, smile and go about her life.

CHAPTER 16

In the spring of 1962, Bob was still a novelist in search of a subject he could seize hold of, beyond the transient ideas he entertained for a time and then dropped. He was at the *Argosy* magazine offices to turn in an article when he finally found the story he could run with. A publicist for an Italian wine company who happened to stop by the offices that day told Bob about an Italian hill town that was said to have hidden its entire treasure—one million bottles of wine—from the Nazis during World War II.

It was one of those tales a novelist yearns for, a great fat multi-layered tale, with peasants outwitting an all-powerful enemy. The true story, of course, was less attractive. The wine had probably been saved through the connivance of a titled industrialist, and the ancient hill town so romantic in Bob's imagination turned out to be a grungy mid-sized industrial city.

But it made no difference. As the weeks passed, Bob began to embroider the story to make it his own. In Bob-like fashion, the facts only served to feed the fiction. At every dinner party, he began expanding on the tale, lacing it with characters who never existed. The story—Bob's story—began to energize our life.

Years later, Bob concocted a legend about writing the legend of *The Secret of Santa Vittoria*:

> I woke one morning in March, there was snow and thunder in the morning, very rare and strange, with the lines "In dreams begin responsibilities" running in my mind. It is a line from Yeats (borrowed, I have since found out, from some obscure Indian poet) that I used to write in all my notebooks when I was in college.

> I began going around New York that morning trying to raise enough money to take me to Italy. I felt the least I could do was look at this place which had become my responsibility.

> When I accumulated $800 beyond the cost of the airfare, I set out for Santa Vittoria.

And so, with everyone's blessing, Bob took off for Italy in search of a town that did not exist. His first letter home, written in pencil forty years ago, still makes me sad.

The last time we were together you looked so tired, so in need of a rest or change that I was really afraid the strain was getting too much. I had to go, of course, but I've worried about you ever since. The fact that the pressure was caused by my not earning anything doesn't help. Also the funny feeling that with all the money you were killing yourself making, we seem somehow worse off.

Do me a favor, right now will you please, take a giant breath, like a two-second vacation and then let your shoulders down. We really are very lucky but life does get away. . .

But then he wrote,

I have to admit that I have, as others before me, become obsessed with the Italian woman. She is truly one of the generous, even glorious creations of the world. This—if you will bear with me—is a highly peculiar way to tell you that I love you very much.

He went on to say that I was beautiful: "You and we have forgotten that at times. You don't believe it always anymore. My fault. Life's fault. Your fault. No one's . . ."

He worried that we were turning middle-aged. I was thirty-one, he was thirty-seven. We had, he said, gone through some hard sailing.

Bob began his Italian journey at the winery, hostage to the promotion man who was determined that Bob glorify his client. Bob had not come to Italy to hang around a label-making machine with a publicist:

My plan now is this: I am going to leave here happily some time tomorrow. The interviews are no good at all. That doesn't matter. In a way I'm glad because the less I rely on reality, the more I can create my own story. I have got to get to central Italy in the Umbrian-Tuscany region; find the ideal town and then stay there for three four five days until I have forced myself to sketch in the entire plot.

When I find it, I will send an address where you can get me. I want to hear all you are doing and thinking.

This letter isn't like me at all, I feel like a flat
stretch runner caught in a steeplechase—totally
out of place, in the wrong race, off the pace. My
clothes somehow are holding up. This is the
dressiest country in the world. Farm boys wear a
coat and tie to go to town for salt.

Bob wandered through "rugged, rocky, menacing, beautiful poor country," searching for a setting for his story. Having never been in Italy before, he began to realize how much he needed to learn and kept extending his stay. When he finally called home, he asked me to buy him ointment to keep his acne in check, pick up the mail in the office that he shared with a drinking buddy, and find him another place to work before he returned.

I was stretched too thin and let him have it. He knew he'd gone too far.

"Back down now, girl," he wrote, and then more loving words. Again he promised to be home in days, then weeks, then a month. He stopped at a regiment of the famed mountain-infantry, the Alpini, and bought Rob one of those wonderful *cappello*, the mountain cap with the raven's feather. As for me,

In Genoa I bought you not just a blouse but, for
the first time, and of course at the risk of seeming

like a lunatic, the sexiest lingerie ever seen—and it
is too small. Don't ask me how I know—I bought it
in a rage to live, a lust for wife—and today I know
as I knew then, it isn't right.

He wrote a sixteen-page handwritten letter to be
shared by all about his trip in a small Fiat, up and over
the Apennines, driving through snow and past grave
markers of those who had died taking the same route. At
the top of the mountain, he realized he was out of gas. "If
anyone had suggested to me that I would coast down
such a clay slick mountain," he wrote, "I would have
wagered my life I would do no such thing."

I was not amused by his reckless ways. I kept his
postcards of Italian pin-ups but I did not like them,
either. In some of his letters, he was trying out sentences
and ideas for the book.

Tonight some little mountain men ate here at the
inn. Men with muscles in their faces. They had
songs, lots of bread, a gallon of wine and a plate of
peas.

At 11:00 I came back from walking the town and
they were unloading a double trailer truck of 100
quart wine jugs, each weighing about 265 pounds.

They would drag the huge bottles to the end of the
truck, jump out, lift the jugs down, carry them into
the store and jump back up onto the truck again.
200 of these jugs.

I never saw people work so hard. Old old people,
women carrying loads one would think cruel on a
mule. One sees old people everywhere. They're
still in the life, they watch the oxen, weed the
grapes, tend the babies, cook—but they have a
place, seem needed.

Tomorrow I will be back in the area of the high hill
towns near Orvieto and then I have to plot my
book rapidly. I have so much stuff, so many notes.

Lots of gypsies here, tell Sarah. And tell her and
the others there are plenty of deserted castles for
all.

Bob's car was robbed in Genoa, and he lost his new
Olivetti with the Italian keyboard. He sat in Orvieto
waiting for mail from home but I didn't yet have his
address. He kept on writing.

This afternoon I decided to walk to an Etruscan tomb. The map was bad and it turned out to be 10 kilometers and no buses on the road and hitch-hiking is unheard of.

Coming back I was exhausted. I had so many excellent ideas along the way I hadn't really felt how far I had gone despite a bad leg, when I fell into a drainage ditch while checking an artichoke patch . . . my notebooks are filling up.

By now he was broke and living on pennies.

I had to trade in your very extravagant sexy underwear but I will find you something else when I get back out of the hill country. Missing you somewhat achingly—I remain yr husband,
                    Bob

Finally—

Here is the good news, I am leaving Orvieto this morning May 17th. I have found the country I was searching for. It's called the Abruzzi—the last place where bear, the boar and the wolf still live. It is high rugged country and a perfect blend of Italy.

Grapes, olives, wheat, wealth and poverty, strong
on tradition and the central battling grounds in
Italian policy. Here is Italy in the rough and in a
nutshell. While not as mountainous as many
regions, it manages to be the place for extreme
partisan activity because of the temperament of
the people.

I'm giving myself three or four days here and then
returning to Rome for a day and then home . . .

Tell Sarah I got her lovely five-page letter on thick
paper. How do you people mail those things for 16
cents? It was good to hear from you all.

He said that he was surprisingly lonely, and a number
of his letters were filled with love and lust. Only one of
my letters to him survived. I wrote that Rob, now seven,
was in love, completely, blushingly, miserably in love. I
had yet to meet the girl. Sarah was wandering around by
herself saying it was awfully lonesome without her father.
And I was lonesome, too.

By the summer of 1962, during another blessed
month on the Cape, Bob was back and conjuring his
imaginary Italian hill town, writing in his notebooks,

talking to the Bartles—to anyone who'd listen—about the novel slowly taking shape in his head. He had spent only five or six disorganized weeks wandering around Italy but he was a brilliant observer and to an untutored ear seemed to have acquired the fluency he needed. Towards the end of the trip, he'd begun to focus on the ancient towns seventy odd miles east of Rome, in the craggy mountains of the Abruzzi.

Moving from one town to the next, Bob studied the relationship between the villagers who lived in the sunlight in the high town above the piazza and those at the bottom of the social order who lived much as they had for a thousand years, in the dank caves beneath the crest of the hill. Drinking wine at a cafe and watching the evening *passeggiata*—the traditional evening stroll around the piazza—he noted the dark-eyed girls walking arm in arm, studiously avoiding the eyes of the young men who were bolder in their gaze. His ears picked up on the sounds of bicycles and ox carts as they moved across cobblestones, and the imperious clack of high-heeled shoes against the stones: all would turn up in his book.

What he didn't hear or see—what he only imagined— also took root. *The fountain of the pissing turtle* appeared in the center of the square, and a water tower emerged on the edge of the town. One night when he was describing Bombolini, his imaginary hero, I asked what

Bombolini would have worn to bed. Bob had no idea. He later said the question cost him a year or two. He began camping out in the cavernous reading room of the New York Public Library at 42nd Street, searching for the small but essential details needed to bring his town and its people to life. All the while, he was making no money, and his desk once again became a repository for unpaid bills.

When Bob was writing *The Great Impostor,* the familiar flickers of literary ambition had surfaced, submerged and resurfaced. At the office he would re-read *Crime and Punishment,* believing he could create a minor psychological classic. But then he'd come home at night, re-line the diaper pail, prioritize the bills and by morning, fixed on the need for the next advance, would hurry to turn out the next chapter. *The Great Impostor* was a commercial success, but Bob always knew he could have done better.

Now he was convinced that *Santa Vittoria* was his last chance to escape from hackdom. We agreed he should give up magazine assignments and concentrate on the book. It was not a realistic decision. I did not make enough to support us all but we felt we had no option. At thirty-seven, Bob was no longer a lad. Dylan Thomas was almost dead at thirty-seven, Bob told me.

"Dylan Thomas drank himself to death," I said. Bob didn't answer.

We set the bar too high. Early one evening, parents of a friend of Jenny's arrived to retrieve their daughter, Harriet. The writer Elizabeth Hardwick with her soft southern voice, tiny ankles, fancy shoes, and cutting wit, and her husband, the poet Robert Lowell, sat on our broken-down couch, while I put Suzy to bed and Bob talked of the book he was trying to write. But when they left, Bob told me he felt like a fraud.

He walked around the book for weeks, for months, too scared to begin. He wrote in his notes, "I have come to be fearful of failure." He was far more unsteady than I knew. Bob spent more and more time writing and rewriting notes to explain why he wasn't writing the book than he did on writing the book. His writing sounded like he was running out the clock.

> What is this day. It is a non-typical Tuesday, a day
> just after the opening of autumn, warm as autumn
> so often is, warm not in the Indian summer way
> but with a last vengeful reminder that summer lies
> still within our hemisphere. It is September 25
> 1962. I can't think on this date of any young man
> who has wasted so many hours, so many minutes

and so many weeks and months and years doing nothing.

I am treading water. If I don't begin to move toward some goal on the horizon soon, I know, as any swimmer knows, that I am going to have to retreat . . . or I am going to go down.

What hurts me is that Judy knows about this state of affairs. In Newtown, when people asked about my book, she was ashamed for me as I was ashamed for myself. She knows when I am writing. On that score: I have so immobilized her about asking about my work that she has learned now to no longer have interest in it.

Bob laid out a schedule for himself. He would write a thousand words a day. There would be no lunches, nothing would be allowed to interfere with his work. At the end of the day, he would summarize what he had done and where he intended to go the next day.

I must set a goal for myself and stick to it. This is my last chance. To fail in this now is to almost tamper with suicide. I will control my drinking.

This is my word and my word is my life. If I fail to live up to this schedule, I will have to leave Judy.

I will live up to this. As best I can I shall cease to lie.

Now damn it, get funny.

I wish the notes had stopped there. But there are pages and pages and more troubling pages about broken vows, drinking bouts, extended notes about a cancer scare. Bob was an unlikely hypochondriac. On the one hand, he was a stoic. He once bet his surgeon that he could have polyps removed from his vocal cords without being sedated or gagging. He succeeded and the surgeon knocked $100 off his bill. But Bob also went through periods when he was convinced he was dying. And when that happened, all his fears became interlaced.

How I have been living as a fearful baby. How I have let almost everyone I know make me fearful. Fearful of dying, I have become fearful of life and then of anyone living it. I have even at times been fearful of my children, fearful that they could see right through me.

As I neglect to create, I must in turn downgrade all creativity to compensate for my lack of it. Last night as I talked to Judy's father about the true face of war, I was ashamed. All right, you're a writer, I said to myself. And listen to you talk with such passion about the infantry. But James Jones wrote the book. I didn't. I didn't write anything.

How long can I excuse myself before myself, before my children, before Judy, before the world. They secretly know I am doing nothing.

Can I do five pages a day no matter what? Do I have the guts to do this come hell or high water, dinner dates, dames, darling children, love of life, of wife, of family. Yesterday I nearly lost Robby, I feared for Sarah, I deplored of Susan.

Oct. 15, 1962. On my word, on my life, a new life.

The next day, the Cuban Missile Crisis would begin.

CHAPTER 17

There were moments that October when I came close to calling Stuart Bartle to tell him Bob was going crazy. Bob said he'd gone through bouts of madness when in combat. He would send his other self into battle while the real Bob Crichton used every trick he knew to stay alive. That seemed to me to be a healthy delusion, far from madness. "How do you define madness?" I'd asked him then. But I still don't know what to make of our flight during the Cuban Missile Crisis. Was that madness? Or was I the one in the grip of delusions?

On Monday evening, October 20th, President Kennedy confirmed the presence of Soviet missile sites in Cuba and went on to declare that we would not shrink from the risk of nuclear war. I could see Bob stiffen. How lightly people seemed to speak of nuclear war. The year before, when Soviet and American tanks had faced off at border crossings between East and West Berlin, war seemed near, and Kennedy all too prepared to use the bomb. Now the country was facing an even graver crisis.

Bob was obsessed with the Kennedys. Reckless men, he called them, boy-men with the bomb. The Kennedys held a curious position in our lives, generating a kind of movie star fantasy that Bob and I disdained while also still drawing us in to a degree. But when the President and his brother dragged their heels over civil rights, or were too bellicose in their responses to the Russians, we felt betrayed.

On Wednesday morning, twenty Soviet ships were reported to be steaming towards a confrontation with the U.S. naval blockade surrounding Cuba. American forces were on the alert and there were rumors of an invasion force being readied in Florida. When Bob and I left for work that morning, clusters of neighbors had collected in the building lobby. There was a kind of a low-level murmuring—*nuclear war, nuclear war. Nuclear war* was a phrase Bob said was too abstract; he said he wished it sounded more frightening.

In the streets, everyone was reading a paper, even people one suspected never read the paper. Standing on the subway platform, Bob began to talk about the flash of the absurd, the man he knew but didn't know who ran a newsstand and had died at the hotel where he had his office. From the first rumors about the Soviet missiles, our conversations were filled with curious unfinished fragments. When we parted at 51st Street, Bob never said a word, just kept moving, slapping a folded *New York Times* against his leg.

On the 25th floor of the Seagram Building on Park Avenue, in the *I've Got a Secret* office, a radio was on. As I began a telephone search for the man who had pushed a peanut up Pike's Peak with his nose, I could hear voices calling for an air strike on Cuba. T.S. Eliot's words echoed in my head: "This is the way the world ends, this is the way the world ends. . ." Years earlier, working with a scientist from Syracuse University, I had written a research paper for Eleanor Roosevelt on the dangers of radioactive fall-out from the atomic bomb tests—the first serious work I'd ever done. I understood what was at stake.

At about 2:30 that afternoon, Bob appeared at my desk, his face blotchy, his voice flat with a disconnected quality I had come to dread. There were no preambles. "If we are going to die," he said, "we're going to die all together." The children were waiting in the car in front of the building with a paper sack of snacks. He'd retrieved Sarah, Rob and Jenny from their classes at Dalton, and collected Suzy from the sitter. He wouldn't sit and wait for the bomb to fall with all of us scattered, each alone and afraid.

We drove up Park Avenue and out of town. Where are we going? Bob wasn't sure. Newtown might or might not be far enough north. My mother-in-law May had long since stocked food and water in the cellar. It was not a time for questions. The children could sense their father's panic, and anything I could say might frighten them even more. On the drive north, it was quiet; we had no radio in the car. Suzy sat on my lap, both of us staring straight ahead.

I had marched in every anti-nuke demonstration but my concerns were of the most mundane, immediate sort. I worried that we would run out of gas. Between us, we had very little cash. I tried to judge from the traffic on the highway if the situation was worsening, but the roads were not unusually crowded and almost every car we passed carried a single man at the wheel. At one point, a jet flew low over our heads. Bob jumped and the car swerved slightly. I wanted to put my hand on his arm but knew he would only shrug it off.

Around five we stopped at a diner in Connecticut where we had been before. The coffee was good, the bathrooms were clean. The six of us lined up on stools at the counter, and it was there that we heard that the Soviet ships had stopped dead in the ocean. The dangers were not over but for a moment, they had eased. Bob and I emptied our pockets, counted up our money and ordered as much food as we could afford. After we had eaten, we turned back to the city.

The following day Bob wrote me a six-page letter defending our flight.

Perhaps I am resenting that my anxiety should be considered to be neurosis. That I am perhaps unbalanced and the others sane while someone tempts Khrushchev / takes a calculated risk that he won't fire his nuclear rockets. . .

If the attack occurred, and don't ever forget in the bright light of today how close a great part of the world knew and felt it was going to occur, then we would just take a side road and keep driving ahead, hoping, and never really knowing what overtook us.

In the case of another alarm, he wrote, he would once again leave with me and our kids. The letter rambled and was less coherent than the quotes I've used suggest. There were pages and pages going back to the Battle of the Bulge, of lying exposed on frozen ground during the horror of artillery attacks. Bob imagined standing in the basement of our apartment building, the children huddled in a corner, convinced they would survive because he wouldn't let them die. Bob said he would not dishonor them with a lie. If the bombs began to fall, he would say to the children, "Hold my hand, come out the door and die with me." He knew he might have over-reacted but didn't think so. The letter ended,

> My anxiety isn't a matter of madness. I don't think
> you have to worry on that scale. In fact it is
> perhaps an overdose of sanity built on experience.

I was of two minds. So often Bob swept us along, breathing magic into the commonplace. But there were also those too-exaggerated moments when pathology seemed to take over. For forty years, I have been afraid I would diminish the one by acknowledging the other, and that's been my dilemma: trying to adjudicate between the Bob who was always pushing at the edge of life to make more of it, and the man who sometimes went too far and couldn't stop himself.

Bob's fears in the fall of 1962 were not irrational and his insistence on bringing us all together *was* an act of love. But he was also within a hair's breadth of losing his wits, and that too was clear. Yet isn't a man facing the end of the world entitled to move to the edge of his emotions as well? When the psychiatrist asked, "Tell me, Mrs. Crichton, when did all of this begin?", Bob had pointed to the War. I had been doubtful. But maybe Bob was right.

The explosion in the coffee shop the year that we married, the countless angry outbursts we worked so hard to forget, Bob's guilt and war dreams, the drinking and his exaggerated startle response, all might have been symptoms of PTSD (post-traumatic stress disorder). The syndrome is said to trigger persistent involuntary re-experiences of traumatic distress: nightmares, flashbacks, irritability, fearfulness, nervous agitation. But until the 1980s, there was no medical confirmation that a trauma sustained in 1944 could force a man to relive the horror of combat over and over, or that a reaction to trauma might literally change the chemistry of the brain.

It was not clear to me or Bob that his experience in combat might lead to depression, heavy drinking, and emotional numbing and detachment, all associated with PTSD. For our entire relationship, there had been spasms of emotional detachment which I always found hurtful and never understood.

In the letter Bob wrote me after the Cuban Missile Crisis, he recalled going over a cliff in a jeep shortly after he came home from the army.

Once again I was in violent danger. And my feeling was one of immense, grave boredom. With reluctance my muscles worked to help myself. I was actually bored as the jeep turned and tumbled down the embankment into the water.

The other morning I recognized that feeling. I was enormously bored and with effort I again stirred myself to accept the challenge my mind at first denied. When I did, perhaps I overreacted.

But to be honest about all this, I don't think I overreacted.

In 1962, I was not as understanding as I wish I had been. I was asking Bob for strength and stability, and these were not his to give. He, of course, was asking the same from me.

CHAPTER 18

The last evening on the Cape, August 1963, out on the beach for one last almost-nighttime walk of the summer, Bob raised Lamumba, a menacing ghost of his own invention—"Lamumba!"—and the children screamed. They always screamed. The sun seemed to hover on the horizon as if waiting for the children to have their fill of terror. Einstein was right. Time was a variable. As the screams turned to laughter, the last light left the sky, and we trudged up the Corn Hill dune for our last night in the Truro cottage.

We traveled home like Okies in our banged-up station wagon. "Waste not, want not," Bob said, packing a box of cornflakes with twenty flakes left, toothpaste tubes with just a squeeze or two remaining, the children's shell collection, snacks for the trip, moss for the terrarium, a laundry bag with wet swimsuits tucked beneath my feet. We had stopped at the sea for one last swim—a bonus swim, Bob said, like stealing an extra day.

On these long trips, Rob would be at the ready, waiting and watching for the radiator to run dry. Our car radiator was always running dry, and when it did, it was

Rob's job to fill canisters with water from a creek or gas station. It never occurred to us that the car might be suffering from neglect. Overheated radiators were the natural course of things where Crichton cars were concerned. Our mental road maps were marked with watering holes along our regular runs: the Bronx River on the Saw Mill Parkway and the river that gave the Hutchinson River Parkway its name.

A wonderful summer led into a terrible fall. Days after we returned from the Cape, the Baptist Church in Birmingham was bombed and the four little girls were killed. As the television cameras studied the scene, we could feel the terror of the children trapped in the church basement, murdered in the sanctuary, children little older than our own. There was no longer any remove, nowhere to hide. The authorities were on the side of evil, and to hold one's tongue was to be complicit with evil.

A few months earlier, watching the evening news with the children around us, with Sarah playing jacks on the floor, we had seen Bull Connor, paunchy cocky Bull Connor, Birmingham's Police Commissioner, unleash his attack dogs and water cannon on young Black demonstrators. Weeks later, a Buddhist monk immolated himself on a Saigon street before our eyes to protest the U.S.-backed government in South Vietnam. Then Diem was murdered, Medgar Evers was murdered, the top of

JFK's head was blown off, and Cronkite cried and Jackie refused to change from her blood-stained pink suit.

The images of death cut grooves in our brains. Strangers in the streets talked of a world gone mad. We ricocheted between conspiracy theories—it was the CIA, it was the Cubans seeking revenge for the Bay of Pigs, it was an international conspiracy, it was a military coup d'état.

Sunday morning in Newtown, Jennifer was curled in the protection of my lap, and we watched as Oswald was shot and killed in the corridor of a Dallas jail by the owner of a strip-joint. No one accepted the story that Oswald's killer was a bereaved patriot. Instead, everyone wondered, who had hired Oswald's killer?

Our friend Fred Freed was working on a documentary about the assassination. Earlier that year, he produced a brilliant three-hour show on the civil rights movement for NBC News. I went to see Fred and asked him for a job. "Not a chance," he said. The work was too demanding for a woman with children, he told me. I finished my sandwich and went back to *I've Got a Secret.*

Money was an endless source of tension between Bob and me. We fought about the food bill, the phone bill, my insistence on taking taxis. One Saturday morning, Bob and I fought over a chicken that I insisted was too old to cook. My extravagance, his penuriousness, my wastefulness, his willingness to gamble, all clung to the skin of a not-too-large dead hen. I called Herbie, confident that our good Jewish butcher who understood writers would never allow us to cook a rancid bird. Herbie suggested we send Rob over with the chicken and so we did. Fifteen minutes later, Herbie called back to say that Bob was right: "Just rub the bird with a bit of lemon and it will be fine." We cooked the chicken that evening and then fought about why we had fought.

Bob always said you knew a marriage was over when a husband told his wife, "I hate the way you eat an olive." At Harvard, he had ended an affair when a woman he was with put out her cigarette in a jar of cold cream. Images of women in Bob's life who had disappointed him seemed to drift around us. The metaphors lingered. A few weeks later, I took a second job.

A second job sounds insane for a woman with four children, one of whom needed special help. But I was in a box and Bob was on the defensive, alluding to a book that still did not exist. I had the mindset of a woman with money, and some of the trappings of money, with my mother's silver and my grandmother's beautiful candelabra and a drawer full of antique jewelry that I seldom wore. But we had nothing in the bank.

Like my parents before me, I operated on the assumption there would be bailout money, that money would come from somewhere. It was not realistic. Long gone was my grandparents' mansion in Scarsdale (the one with the eleven servants or was it twelve?. My mother, who long ago had become a regular at pawn shops, now ran a flower shop on St. Thomas. My father was ill; he had spent years struggling to keep up appearances, first in Beverly Hills, now on East 57th Street. And although a fractional share of the Broadway production of *The Sound of Music,* an anniversary gift from Uncle Dick, paid for our month on the Cape each summer, other family handouts were uncertain and our debts were climbing.

My second job entailed writing a daily three and a half-minute essay for *Dimensions of a Woman's World,* a radio show produced by CBS News. I loved the job even though my schedule brooked on the absurd. After the children went to bed, I would settle down at my Olympia portable, our round marble-topped table in the dining alcove still sticky from supper, and write as Bob washed the dishes.

My work schedule now dominated our life. There was little time to spare. Monday nights I always stayed late for the taping of *I've Got a Secret.* But working on the radio show gave me a professional toe-hold in the real world, even if I didn't always know what to make of it.

In December, Betty Friedan and I interviewed each other while Christmas shopping at a third-hand fur store on the Lower East Side. Betty, who had just written *The Feminine Mystique,* interviewed me for an article about the problems of working mothers, while I interviewed her to explore the implications of her book on our real, every-day lives. Hunting through bins of discarded furs, ratty neck pieces and silver fox boas, I found Jennifer a superb white ermine jacket with matching muff that I suspect was really rabbit. I don't remember if Betty Friedan was as lucky. But when we parted, she had the material she needed for her essay while I remained perplexed about her book.

The Feminine Mystique was centered on what Friedan described as *the problem that had no name.* She wrote about dissatisfied housewife-mothers who'd been taught they would reach Nirvana once they had families of their own, women who sublimated their personal desires and then found themselves with unarticulated and unacceptable longings. She wrote of women who, at the end of a day, were afraid to ask "the silent question, 'Is this all?'"

I was confused by the book, confused by my own life. I'd become the main breadwinner for a family of six, but my focus was still on Bob's career. I flirted with the idea of working to fulfill my inner needs, but Bob's ambitions came first. The conflict in my life was over his writer's block and our pressing need to make more money. My personal frustration had to do with time—free time, play time, time for the children, time for myself. Standing in front of the laundry machines in the basement at midnight was my idea of hell.

A poll in the 1950s had revealed that many women would have preferred to have been born a man, but I was not among them. I puzzled over a quote by Kierkegaard I'd read in Simone de Beauvoir's *The Second Sex*: "What a misfortune to be a woman! And yet the misfortune, when one is a woman, is at bottom not to comprehend that it is one." I was still trying to create the home I'd never had, trying to be the mother I had always wanted, striving to preside over the good and happy kingdom of contented children.

I knew enough not to tell Friedan, but in some interior corner of my brain, I still assumed that every man in my life was smarter-brighter-stronger-quicker than I was—just generally superior. De Beauvoir was outraged at being classed as a member of the Second Sex, but I was not. I still could not envision going to a woman doctor, a woman surgeon. Lawyers, doctors, even journalists were men. When Fred Freed turned me down because work on a news documentary was too demanding for a woman with a family, I thought he was right.

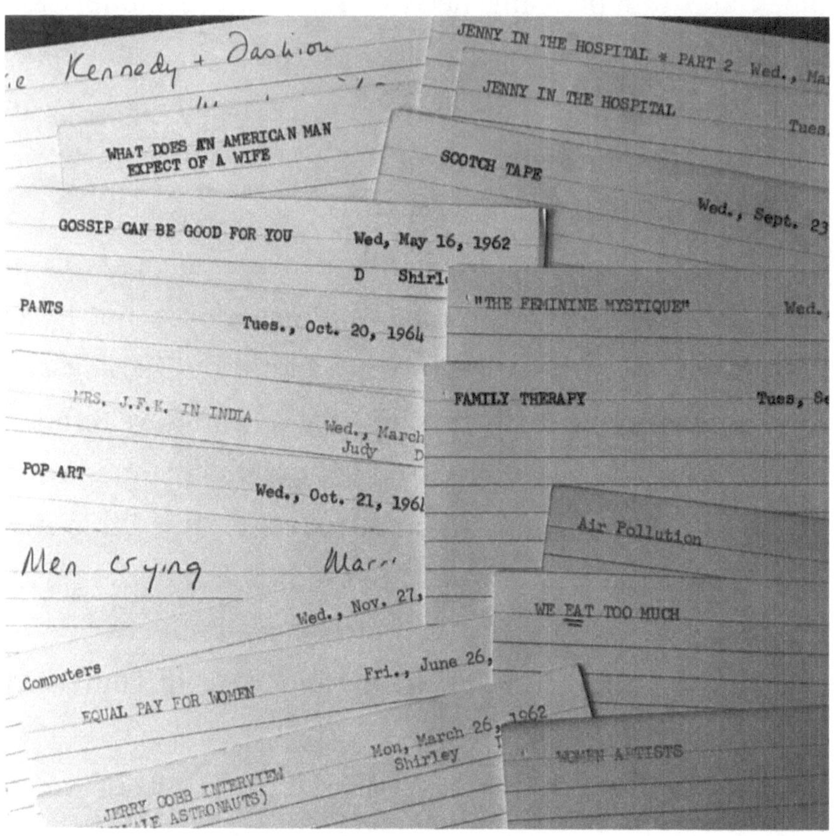

Index cards with some topics covered on Dimensions of a Woman's World: family therapy, men crying, "we eat too much," air pollution, equal pay for women, The Feminine Mystique, pop art, pants—and Scotch tape

Sexism? It had yet to dawn on me. As a term, sexism did not even yet exist. Living in an interracial world, I had become sensitized to the problems of race but not to the problems of women. The teachings of my childhood still clung to my brain like barnacles. I can't remember what I wrote about Friedan, but I know I didn't recognize her as the seminal figure she was.

The most liberated friend I had was Betty Furness. Betty had shaped her own life, was openly ambitious, dependent on no one, and took lovers the way men did—simply for fun. Betty and I had met in the late 1930s when I was nine. She was a starlet in her early twenties, married to the composer John Green. I can see her in my family's New York City living room, wearing a short skirt and a bird on a hat that was tipped over one eye. She was small and narrow, with perfect hands and an imperfect nose, and I could hear her laugh long after I was sent off to bed.

I was seventeen when Betty reappeared, dead broke, with her career going nowhere. She had come east from Hollywood to reinvent her life. Settling into the apartment with my mother and me, she slept in my father's recently abandoned bed, and in her brisk and efficient way, swept the bitterness out of the room. There was a take-no-prisoners directness about Betty, and she set out to establish her television career as though she were mounting a military campaign. A card table set up in my mother's bedroom became her office. In slanted handwriting as distinctive as her brisk, throaty voice, Betty noted details of every phone call, every interview, the name of every secretary. In a matter of weeks, she landed a small role on *Studio One*, an early dramatic series sponsored by Westinghouse, which led to her being hired as the Westinghouse spokeswoman.

On live feed, in a precursor of what would be called infomercials, Betty opened and closed refrigerator doors, and demonstrated vacuum cleaners, with a crisp, professional yet relatable manner that connected with the viewers. When Westinghouse sponsored the 1952 presidential conventions, Betty became as famous as the newscaster Walter Cronkite and may have made more money.

Betty once took me to a party when I was quite young and pointed out three or four men in the room she had gone to bed with. Betty was an absolutely brilliant flirt and over time, there was a senator and journalists, actors and composers and finally a husband whom she really loved. What never occurred to either of us at the time was that Betty was also just plain brilliant. When Betty and I began *Dimensions of a Woman's World,* Betty rejoiced that we were both inching into the news business, even if the newsmen didn't know we were there.

Bob felt Betty was indulgent and encouraged my extravagance. Betty felt that Bob was too tough on me. Both of them were right. I'd take off for work early, leaving Bob with Suzy, gazing out the window, waiting for the sitter.

"You march out and take a cab," Bob wrote me. "That's fine. It is your money. Let's face it. I'm forced to increasingly think that way. Don't tell me you don't think so either."

Holidays and Christmas were irritants cutting into his momentum. On the back of an envelope, Bob kept track of the hours he actually spent working: too few. He was hurt that I had stopped asking him about his progress. But I no longer believed there was any progress and this he probably knew. Bob wrote again about his fear of failure. I had come to be fearful of his failure as well.

CHAPTER 19

At times, both Bob and I hid behind Bob's charm. It was easy to do. Even his notes in his notebooks were part of that dance, the extended notes that served as warm-up exercises to stave off the real writing he wanted to avoid. Even after all these years, I sense their charm as well as the fear and avoidance that didn't always stay below the surface.

Today is the first day of Spring. Usually this always has a good deal of meaning to me, the beginning of a new era, the end of another. But as long as the book isn't done, there is no end or beginning. The book dictates time—post book, pre-book.

I wrote a four page letter to Alistair Horne, author of *The Price of Glory*, the sickening story of Verdun. Essence was that the story of Verdun, instead of making me feel better, only reaffirms the fact that mankind has the potential to destroy itself.

If nations allowed themselves to go to war again after Verdun, there is nothing to hold this same kind of man from eventually employing atomic weapons. If the insanity of mankind at the present were reasonably new, one might hope that certain measures might be found to control it. But Verdun proves that this insanity is in a long, honored tradition.

I am somewhat hung over this morning since, after not drinking for three days, I had so worked myself into an intellectual aggressiveness that I felt a drink might soften me. It didn't help.

Poor Judy and I had a fight about, as usual, her working all through the evening. I feel that when someone comes to get shortchanged, it is me who does the paying. Until the book is done and I have my advance, and Judy can drop back to one job, this fight, I suspect, will continue to emerge.

This afternoon, before lunch, I sat down and wrote myself a three page letter about the reason for all the fights Judy and I have been having. I am afraid that I see it as a struggle, momentarily for her affections. She is somewhat in love with _______________ [left blank], not seriously in love, but in love. The infatuation comes at a bad time. The time I was loved most is the time I needed it less.

I don't know whether I should or shouldn't say what I know. Some truths are better left unsaid. So I write this and perhaps it can stay here.

If only my book were done and I had my advance and I could be my own free confident man again since it is, indeed, more fun.

Bob noted that my attention had strayed, and it had. When Bob dallied in Europe, I turned around with all the passion and fury of the insecure and began a flirtation of my own. Three steps forward, four back. It didn't help, of course. I was still too vulnerable to recognize that, in many ways, Bob was as vulnerable as I was.

On a winter morning well before dawn, Suzy woke us to say that Jenny had to go to the bathroom but was too sick to walk. A few hours later, Jenny was operated on for a ruptured appendix. Impaled with tubes, drips, a catheter, both arms tied down to keep the gear in place, she was the grayest, most fragile seven-year-old I had ever seen. For weeks she hardly spoke, never cried, kept her head turned towards the wall. Even her eyes were barely responsive.

One night, after a third operation was required to halt the peritonitis infection threatening Jenny's life, Bob and I were called into the dimmed corridor outside her room. The doctor had few words of comfort. We could hear what he was saying but neither of us could absorb the fact that Jenny was so dangerously ill. There's no corner of the soul prepared to consider the death of a child. A nurse offered to bring us coffee but we couldn't accept her solicitous ways. We stood together looking out the window, waiting for morning.

Then at some point the next day, Jen's blood count began to improve and the doctors grew cautiously optimistic. But Jenny kept her face turned to the wall. On paper she was gaining, but she refused to respond—for hours, then for days, for too many days. During grand-rounds one morning, a senior doctor explained to a cohort of interns that for reasons no one understood, Jennifer had been unable to turn the corner. The phrase was like a lash across my face.

Then a young woman intern, the only woman among the doctors, broke from the pack. Kneeling in the narrow passage between the wall and Jenny's bed, her eyes level with Jenny's, she asked the question that none of us had

had the sense to ask. "What can we do to help you, Jenny? What can we do to help?"

In a voice so soft it almost wasn't there, Jenny answered, "I want to suck my thumb." Within moments, an IV was shifted to Jenny's leg, her right arm was freed, and her thumb was in her mouth. She had needed to retreat before she could muster the strength to move forward. Days later, Bob and I took her home together.

During the dark days when Jenny was so ill, and I was all but living at the hospital, Sarah brought home a letter from her fourth grade teacher. Our lovely brilliant daughter with the long, long legs had been cutting up in class, and Bob, on his own, wrote the teacher about the mitigating circumstances in Sarah's life.

Jennifer was very sick. This meant all the attention went to her. As you may know, until I finish a long novel I am working on, my wife has had to hold two jobs. Sarah was left to shift for herself. I hope she does improve, I expect her to. But if she doesn't, will you please let us know. It ordinarily isn't like Sarah . . .

Weeks later Bob explained that he'd elected not to tell me about the incident because he feared I might overreact. He assumed that "such a thing would not occur again in a girl like Sarah," and the matter had gone far enough, Sarah had been sufficiently punished simply by having to carry the letter home. But I was deeply shaken, furious at being excluded. Had I become such a dragon lady that Sarah and Bob needed to keep such a matter to themselves?

In a five-page letter to me, Bob expanded on his decision.

> Talking in class when it interrupts the class or
> upsets the teacher is largely anti-social behavior.
> You can punish the act if you wish, but far better is
> to find the way to get the person to adopt social
> behavior again.

Bob believed we were all born with an instinct to do good and that the business of society, and certainly of parents, was to reinforce those instincts.

> I feel that children raised in this fashion will not be
> lax. Far from it. They will not look to any other
> yardstick but their own highly developed instincts

for social, creative behavior, to know what needs to be done.

Bob's concerns about me were buried on the fourth page of the letter.

> I feel that recently you have had a tendency to be severe at times, with not always the best results. Because you have been working so hard, you have suffered a continuous guilt feeling that perhaps you have over-neglected the development of the children and fear that they are getting away from you.

> I don't think you have any need to be guilty. The children are getting enough guidance and love. I wish then that you would relax more about yourself and your role. If you teach children how to respect life, and respect each other and respect themselves (not feel guilty or ashamed about themselves, not to have to defend themselves against some presumed inner core of evil we all are presumably burdened with), you cover 98% of all human situations.

And this can be taught in one minute a day because it is an <u>attitude</u>. It is transmitted without teaching and lectures. It comes with life.

As such I think we've done a good job. I'm quite at ease about it. These kids hunger to be good, be creative, be useful, be admired, respected. Of course they're going to do wrong things but there's no use to imply that they have some kind of evil within. The only sensible thing is to see how they can avoid doing these things again. And it doesn't really entail punishment but enlightenment.

Bob was right, of course, and he and I held the same core beliefs. But there were times when guilt and fear bred severity. I would hear my mother's voice, cold and mean as frost, leap from my throat. I understood it was the uncommon husband and father who would craft such a missive.

The following afternoon, Sarah did her homework on my office floor. It was neither the first nor the last time, but her presence that afternoon was a comfort to us both. And one afternoon that spring, Rob brought home a small picture book he'd made in school. "Happiness," he wrote, "is dragging your blanket into the living room. Happiness is dandelions."

Happiness is being pulled back to the central core of life. On Mother's Day, the children presented me with a good conduct medal Bob had found for me in a pawn shop.

Although Suzy lived in some limbo land no one could define, she too hungered to be good, to be creative, useful, admired. She loved being sent on family missions from one room to the next, but she couldn't stack blocks the way a six-year-old should. She went up and down stairs with her right foot leading, and she rarely understood the need for social boundaries. She would approach a stranger in the park to say that she had to go to the bathroom or to ask for a piece of candy. She was still our gentle child but there were flashes of stubbornness. I liked to think those were a mark of increasing independence, but I wasn't sure.

After school the older children would take her downstairs to play in front of the building, but she interrupted their games and it was hard for them to mind her for long. Our deal was simple: the kids would bring her back upstairs to the housekeeper before they lost their patience. No one in the outside world could tell how old this child was. She was short for a Crichton, small for her age, but she had a kind of intuitive wisdom that caught one off guard. "Why are you so sad?" she would ask, when you thought you'd managed to conceal your emotional indisposition.

Suzy had begun to steal food—from our plates, from the refrigerator, even from the garbage can. I attributed her behavior to an unsatisfied need for love and attention: guilt, guilt, a hundred times guilt. Suzy and I went to see Peter Neubauer, considered the leading child psychiatrist in the city. Dr. Neubauer's reputation would be destroyed when it emerged he was the mastermind of the twins and triplets studies that purposely separated babies up for adoption in order to study their development in isolation.

For this visit, I wasn't sure why we were there. More for me, perhaps, than for Suzy. I felt the need to test my own thoughts, my own responses. I was haunted by the stories about Bob's brother Billy who developed such a terrible temper he had to be sent away. But I couldn't ask Neubauer about the connection between Billy and Suzy. I didn't have enough facts to even frame a question.

Suzy enjoyed the visit, loved the attention, and leaped to answer Neubauer's questions. "Did I do it right?" she asked. He tried to tell her there was no right or wrong answer but she didn't believe him. She was terrible with numbers but good with words. Her test scores were all over the map. Neubauer did not believe she was really retarded. "She's borderline," he said. But borderline equaled slow and slow was almost retarded. He also questioned the diagnosis of myasthenia gravis. He was the second doctor to do so in as many months.

That night Bob and I decided to experiment and stop giving Suzy the neostigmine which she had been taking since seeing Dr. Osserman all those years ago. The following day, we watched and waited. She didn't seem unduly sleepy, her muscle tone was no worse, her soft round arms no more ineffectual than they were the day before. I stayed home in case she had a reaction but there was none.

That night, we threw away the medication and never saw or spoke to Dr. Osserman again. But now, when people asked about our youngest child, we didn't know what to say. It was clear that something was amiss, that Suzy was a bit off, like a spinning top at the moment it begins to lose its balance but when there's still a chance that it might right itself again.

There had been comfort in giving Suzy's condition a name, even one that was incorrect. It would be twenty years before we would have an accurate diagnosis. In the late 1980s, Suzy was diagnosed with a genetic disorder, Prader-Willi Syndrome. Short stature, uncontrolled appetite, and mixed cognitive strengths and deficits were its signature. Suzy was thrilled to have a proper diagnosis and to find "my people" in a group home for other young and not-so-young people with Prader-Willi. By that time, Suzy had been hospitalized three or four times in psychiatric hospitals. She needed an explanation for why she was as she was, even more than we did.

But now we enrolled Suzy in a small progressive private school and sent her to a tutor who specialized in children with learning problems. We didn't care if she was behind, as long as she could learn at her own rate, whatever that might be. As for me, I came to realize I loved this child of mine without effort, without bitterness, just as I had the other three.

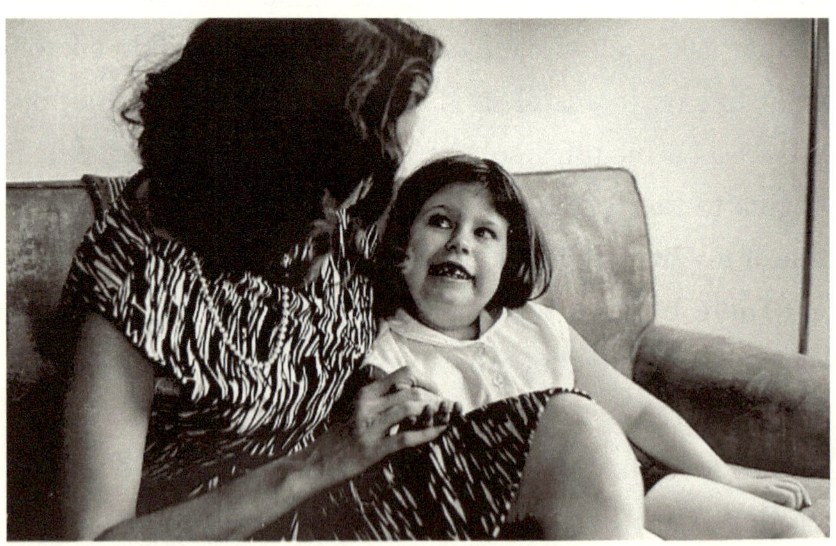

CHAPTER 20

Fortune can turn on trivial events. Bob and I were in a taxi on Madison Avenue, inching north in a torrential rain, when I saw Tony—handsome Tony Schulte whom I had known since childhood and our afternoons at Viola Wolff's dancing lessons, never disheveled then or now—standing on a corner beaten down by rain. Nothing in that soggy encounter suggested he would be the agent of transformation in Bob's life. But my childhood friend was now in publishing at Simon & Schuster, and a week later we went to the Schultes' for dinner.

When Bob began telling Tony the story of Santa Vittoria, it was clear he'd found his voice. Bob was immersed in the tale, spinning out the details vividly and full of life. All through the telling, Tony was listening. Tony was a superb listener, and Bob was inspired. The tension was growing, the Germans were closing in, the wine had yet to be hidden, and the Nazis were laying out their tools for torture.

The following week, Bob turned in a chunk of the book to his agent, and it was the first time I knew for certain that a manuscript actually existed. A few days later, Tony sent him a note from Simon & Schuster saying "Welcome aboard." Bob had a publisher, an advance, and a gifted young editor named Robert Gottlieb.

With Tony Schulte at the Santa Vittoria book party

If we had sent to an alchemist for the perfect editor, he could not have produced better. Gottlieb was as playful as Bob, had read as much or more, and could read even faster. Gottlieb was a master of the absurd. He knew the repositories for the best kitsch in the city and we would go window shopping in search of Jesus figures with eyes that followed you across a room. When Gottlieb was fortunate enough to find an item with absolutely no redeeming esthetic features, he took it home.

Most important, Gottlieb was comforting. He had a gift for intimacy that brushed beyond defenses. Little was out of bounds. He called Bob "Bobbo" and the children "dear ones," and brought a slew of people into our lives: beautiful Maria Tucci, who would become his wife, a talented actor who was gentle and funny and intuitive, and totally without malice, and Nina Bourne, almost otherworldly and ageless with her magically twisting-and -turning bun piled on her head. Nina designed brilliant advertising campaigns and, along with Bob Gottlieb and Tony Schulte, formed the talented triumvirate at Simon & Schuster.

For the first time in years, Bob and I both felt confident about the future, and the two of us began having fun again. We would have dinners with the Gottliebs, often spending our weekends together, and under Gottlieb's persuasion, Bob began to finish *The Secret of Santa Vittoria*. His old insecurities still surfaced but he worked his way through them. In a notebook, Bob wrote, "By chance I saw an editor's note about the book that said, 'This is really very good, you know' and I felt the note was a plant, a kind of editor's water wings designed to buoy me up for a sea of revisions." I'd yet to see a page of the book, but for the first time in years, I knew that Bob was making progress.

Then, in March 1965, there was a letter from the Dalton School.

Dear Mr. Crichton,

I am sorry to tell you that the Scholarship Committee of the Board of Trustees has considered your application for Rob, Sarah and Jennifer and has decided that it cannot make an award to them at this time. Your application does not establish serious enough financial needs.

From the time Sarah started school in 1959, the children had received partial scholarships. It had been common practice in those days for private schools to support artistic families and I met with the treasurer of Dalton to ask for one more year of grace. The scholarship committee assumes, he told me, that anyone who had gone to Harvard could be making $40,000 a year by now. It was clear the treasurer and his committee thought that Bob Crichton was a goof-off. The book advance from Simon & Schuster had settled our debts but we had nothing left to pay the school bills. Somehow I would have to find a way to make even more money. But for the first time in years, everything seemed possible.

For almost four years, my father had asked about the progress of Bob's book and every time he asked I would say it's coming, it's coming. Over time it had become the forbidden question. But early in 1966, with the shift in my voice and the change in Bob's demeanor, the book once again became the focus of our conversations. Ben now lived in New York. He had produced two excellent documentary series for ABC, one on Winston Churchill and the other on FDR.

But before he could take on another project, Ben was operated on for colon cancer. A year later, he could not get back into the life. His energy level was low and his face still gray. Broke and discouraged, he took a job in the publicity office that handled the Rodgers and Hammerstein account, and for months tried to advance Dick's ambitions while burying his own.

Now over our weekly lunch in a restaurant he could not afford, Ben suggested that he would like to produce the film version of *Santa Vittoria*. It was a miserable moment, for him and for me. I could not compose my face. I knew he was grabbing for a lifeline, but I could not ask Bob to place his book in my father's hands. The pause between Ben's question and my answer was long—too long—and a waiter used the quiet to sweep crumbs from the table.

"You should read the book first," I said.

My father nodded and we never discussed the subject again. A few months later, Ben was dead. It would have been so easy to have comforted him with a lie.

There's a photo of Ben taken some time before World War I. He was on his way to Europe with his family aboard one of the great passenger liners. His father, a handsome, tight-lipped man, had come across an empty cage for a large dog, about four feet high. He called for his son, placed him in the cage, closed the door and took the photo. There's no clowning in this snapshot. My father, who was about five at the time, is wearing a formal coat and wide-brimmed hat and is clearly frightened, staring out through the bars with a sad and sober look that he never lost.

The night Ben lay dying, his wife of fourteen years, a beautiful, bright and foxy woman named Wilhelmina, unwilling or unable to travel with him any further, left his bedside at Sloan Kettering, went home, took a sleeping pill and turned off the phone. My father died alone.

Just days before on a Sunday afternoon, I'd been sitting beside his bed with the *New York Times*. Hoping to distract him as well as myself, I began to read aloud. It was not a help, and after a few minutes, I put the paper down. My father pulled his arm out from under the covers in a motion that was painful and slow. I placed my hand on his, and it was all the contact either of us needed.

"It's all right," he said. "It's all right."

As he drifted off, I thought of the rare but wonderful Sunday afternoons when we'd go to Loew's, the great movie palace on 72nd Street, to see Fred Astaire and Ginger Rogers. Then walking home, my father would whistle the score. He had a lovely whistle.

Early January, Bob began rewriting the book, four hundred and forty-seven pages. Over the next two months he lost twenty pounds, began to feel small, and suffered what he called the phenomenon of the missing drink. Each time he made a drink, his glass would suddenly be empty, leading him to make another. Bob was on one continuous high. He would come home at night and play boogie-woogie on our old upright piano. He would get that left hand going and the kids would dance and he was Big Bill Broonzy or Fats Waller singing "I love ya but ya feets too big."

He was in one of those moods where there was nothing he couldn't do. There was an accident at 125th Street, a car had spun out of control, and Bob waded into the crowd, discovered a man with a mangled leg and controlled the bleeding until the ambulance arrived.

One morning as we were getting on the express train at 125th Street, a small Black girl squeezed in between us.

As the doors closed, we could hear the girl's mother screaming from somewhere on the platform. Bob put his head out a window and shouted, "Stay right there! I'll bring her back!" He picked up the terrified child hoping to soothe her, but she cried all the louder and pounded on his chest. At 59th Street, with the little girl still screaming and trying to wrest free, Bob made his way from one platform to another. We often speculated about what would have happened if a tall Black man had tried to rescue a protesting Sarah, carrying her weeping from one subway car to the next. But no one stopped Bob as he carried the little girl through the crowded station onto the uptown train and back to her mother.

The day Bob finished *Santa Vittoria*, March 7, 1966, he turned the manuscript over to Gottlieb at the Simon & Schuster offices. He was jogging up Lexington Avenue to my office in the Seagram Building when just a block or two away, he collapsed. Taking refuge in a phone booth, he called me to say he was suffering a heart attack. While I ran to find him, a colleague called Bob's doctor, and by the time I reached the phone booth, Bob was on the phone with his doctor.

The episode turned out to be more frightening than dangerous. Bob was suffering from a form of fibrillation, a rapid heartbeat accompanied by a sudden and dramatic weakness. Fatigue, alcohol, tension—all had taken their toll. An anxious hour or two in the doctor's office and we headed home, Bob's electrocardiogram scrolled in my arms. Some blocks south of La Salle Street we opened the windows of the cab, and the electrocardiogram began to unwind and, as if taking on a life of its own, floated slowly out the taxi's window. Both of us were so exhausted, all we could do was watch it sail away.

Helen Marcus—a friend from my girlhood and a superb photographer—waited at the apartment. She'd come to take the official photo for the book jacket. Bob took a shower, put on his best sports coat and with the children watching, faced the camera with a bemused expression.

We were, he said, "home free."

Four years of tension, too many arguments, one erratic heartbeat, and now eight pounds of manuscript sat on our marble table. I wasn't as generous as I might have been. When would I have time to read it, this book on which our entire future seemed to rely? I was too scared. Bob was scared, too. We stalled over supper, stalled over the dishes, Bob walked the dog far longer than was needed, the building across the way went dark, and then there was nothing for it. I curled up on the couch and began.

The dedication read,

To Judy who for four years
led two lives and sometimes three lives
so that I could write these lives.

I hadn't needed to be scared. I read the book until morning, going back every so often to run my fingers over the dedication, then inching back into the story, sometimes the reader, sometimes the wife. Not since those early drafts of his Queens memoir, *The Minnow Fishers,* had Bob achieved the level of lyricism and humor that was at the heart of *Santa Vittoria.* This was a rich, fat, complicated multi-layered novel, and tougher than I expected.

Bob had created a narrator for the novel, an alter ego named Roberto Abruzzi, an Italian-American crewman on a B-24 bomber who has participated in one of those unmarked wartime atrocities that so obsessed Bob. After Roberto's plane, the Odessa Darling, scores a direct hit on Santa Vittoria's cathedral, Roberto joins with other crewmen in kicking smaller bombs out of the bomb bay onto a soccer field. As the plane circles the field, Roberto watches as a boy, running with a soccer ball in his arms, is consumed by flames. And that is the end of Roberto's war. He steps through the bomb bay, pulls his rip cord and lives to relive the horror of his actions.

I wanted to talk to Bob about Roberto, and went into the bedroom, but Bob held on to sleep and I went back to the book.

The names of Bob's characters were wonderful. He had always had fun with names: Caterina Malatesta, Giovanni Pietrosanto, Luigi Casamassima (a name he had seen on a garbage truck in Greenwich Village). There were times in the book when I wondered if he was writing about us, the meeting between Caterina and the wounded Tufa: "There was an awareness of each other that was so acute and powerful that it went beyond anything we know as love...they were able to share things with each other at once that they have never been able to share before." And there were Bob Crichton excursions, as elaborate as the scroll work on the cathedral door.

At breakfast, the six of us drank orange juice out of wine glasses as I told the children the story of Santa Vittoria, how men, old as well as young, and women and children had passed a million bottles of wine down a mountainside in a single day and night, so the wine could be hidden in a cave and sealed with wine-stained bricks. I explained how, in the face of torture and reprisals, not one person in Santa Vittoria revealed the secret to the

Germans. Finally, I read them the very end of the novel—the end of the War—when the Royal Sutherland Highlanders arrive in the town, hot, tired and thirsty, and ask for a drink. "Tell them this, Roberto," the mayor shouts. "Tell them God yes, we have something to drink."

On our fifteenth wedding anniversary, a columnist for *The New York Post* reported, "People are beginning to talk about Robert Crichton's *The Secret of Santa Vittoria*." A few weeks later, Daphne Du Maurier sent Bob Gottlieb a letter, "You are so right to love this book. It is superb. Will that do for a quote?" It had been hard slogging, but as Bob said, from here on out, it would be easy sailing.

We didn't quite know what to do with ourselves that summer. With the publication date set for September 1966, we couldn't spend a month on the Cape in a house without a phone. Vacation was upon us when we rented an old rose-covered cottage on a sleepy side street in Sag Harbor. That the house came with a bocce court and a grape arbor seemed only fitting. The children loved the small-town freedom, the safe narrow streets where they could ride their bikes, the Whaling Museum open on rainy days, the movie house that charged only a quarter.

Bob with bocce balls in the Sag Harbor backyard

The rooms of the cottage were small, the ceiling and doorjambs low. "Six brain cells dead!" Bob shouted each time he hit his head. The phone rang often: calls from Simon & Schuster, updates on how many books were shipped to stores, Hollywood agents hot on the trail. The

Gottliebs came for the weekend, the house was always crowded. Bob became obsessive about his bocce score, playing till sundown in a white knit shirt with strong brown arms. Fatigue had left his face.

Then at 11:45 p.m. on August 17th—I know because I made a note of the time—Judy Prince, married to the Broadway director Hal Prince, called to read Bob the review of *Santa Vittoria* that would appear the next day in *The New York Times*. The opening lines read, "If I had my way, the publication of Robert Crichton's brilliant novel would be celebrated with fanfares of trumpets, with the display of banners and with festivals in the streets. This is an irresistibly engaging, hilariously funny book. It bubbles with gaiety and wit, bursts with laughter and throbs with the sheer joy of life."

Before breakfast, Bob got on his bicycle to pick up copies of *The Times* for us to hold in our hands. The phone started early and rang all day: Dorothy Rodgers, Gottlieb, Betty Furness, friends from the office, Bob's brother Andy, the agent from the coast. Hal Prince called to say that the film director Alan Pakula was interested in the book. But Stanley Kramer was offering $300,000, with bonuses to boot.

That night, at a rambling seafood restaurant over-looking the bay, trying to find our emotional sea legs, we ran into Elaine and John Steinbeck. Elaine was a small pretty southern woman whom I'd known when she was married to the actor Zachary Scott. Steinbeck was outsized, rough-skinned and charming. Bob and Steinbeck, big men both, drank to life, drank to writing, drank to any excuse there was to drink. Steinbeck was generous and picked up the check.

It was clear our life was about to change. I went to sleep hoping Bob would now relax and accept himself as the very good writer that he was.

Back home in our La Salle Street apartment, the phone continued to ring: friends from Portsmouth Priory, from Bronxville, strangers who found our number in the telephone book. Bob used to quote J.D. Salinger's Holden Caulfield who said, "What knocks me out is a book that, when you're all done reading it, you wish the author that wrote it was a terrific friend of yours and you could call him up on the phone whenever you felt like it."

There were daily reports from Tony Schulte or Gottlieb that they'd gone back for another printing and then another. *Time* magazine said the book was the funniest war novel since *Mister Roberts:* "A hilarious Iliad . . . Crichton tells his story with grace, pace, warmth and a wonderful freewheeling wit that skips among the vineyards like an inebriated billy goat."

On September 13th the children received a telegram from Gottlieb:

Santa Vittoria number eight on next Sundays best seller list. Please inform parents. Gottlieb.

*Maria Tucci, Bob Gottlieb and Elizabeth Hardwick
at the Santa Vittoria book party*

At the Simon & Schuster Book and Author Lunch, in the grand ballroom of the Waldorf-Astoria, Bob shared the platform with Cornelia Otis Skinner and Garson Kanin. I walked across the lobby past the posters of Robert Crichton, bestselling author, and remembered the times in the early 1950s when Bob and I were too broke to go to the movies and would spend Saturday nights sitting in the Waldorf lobby, inventing stories for each other about the stiff-faced men and overly-groomed women. Now we were the people the people watchers in the Waldorf lobby watched, with Bob striding ahead of me as he so often did.

The whirlwind that began in Sag Harbor continued through the fall, with a torrent of reviews, letters, requests for appearances on the *Today* and *Tonight Shows*, as well as the Dalton Book Fair where he went from supplicant to honored parent in just a few months. We were invited to dinner by people we scarcely knew and we invited some of them back. And then one night I found this note on our kitchen table:

I am not a playhorse I am not a showhorse
I'm a very serious person who needs serious people
I've reached a stage in life where I don't want to
play at it . . .

For a few months, Bob turned into one of the big time spenders. On one extraordinary giddy day in early fall, he sold the book club rights and paperback rights and closed a movie deal with producer Stanley Kramer. A friend talked him into buying a European-style double vent suit from Meledandri and the most beautiful sports coat either of us had ever seen. Bob took me to lunch in the kind of restaurant we never went to—a fancy French restaurant in the east 60s—where over wine and escargot, he made me blush.

After lunch we went to Georges Kaplan, the furrier, where Bob settled into a boudoir chair, legs splayed out over the thick pale rug, while Kaplan showed us the collection. Bob bought me two fur coats in less than an hour: a poplin raincoat lined in alpaca and a silver fox with a red satin lining.

*Camping it up in my silver fox coat; Betty
Furness embroidered the pillow with the
opening lines of the Times' rave review*

We took a taxi home with the outsized boxes, back to La Salle Street to collect the children. Jenny remembers Bob coming home throwing dollar bills into the air. That it never happened doesn't make the memory less real. I can see Bob doing a little dance on the sidewalk in front of Sam Goody's, a quick shuffle and finger snap, and then once again he was buying us each a record album of our choice. It was now a tradition. Then dinner at a Chinese restaurant (fancier than our local Shanghai Cafe on 125th Street, and finally to the Kips Bay Theater to see *The Endless Summer,* a movie about surfing which Sarah reviewed for the Dalton Middle School magazine. Several weeks later, Sarah's review was quoted in a huge ad in the Times: "There is not a moment of dullness throughout the whole picture, a spectacular job. Everybody, students and teachers, must see *The Endless Summer*! It is something that never has been done before and this time it was done just right."

As fall began to slide into winter, Bob was exhausted. He'd been on a letter-writing binge, composing letters for critics who had reviewed the book. He knew it was against the law of the literary land but he didn't care. He wrote to Granville Hicks, an old friend of his father's,

The first reaction I had on reading your review
was that I wished Kyle were still here to read it.

I've had that feeling a few times but this time it was very strong. . .

You occupied an image in our minds when we were kids. I remember well once when we stopped at your farm which was situated somewhere between Rome and Troy. You were getting by living very cheaply and thus able to work on a book and survive, and Kyle gave us a lecture after that. It was a romantic vision of the writer that has never quite left me.

Now Bob was a writer, and a success to boot.

***

CHAPTER 21

Success: what a strange business. It was not a word Bob applied to himself or a condition he had sought. All he had ever wanted was to write a good book and make enough money to buy the time to write another. He was embarrassed by all the talk about the money. Every deal he signed—the book clubs, the paperback sale, the motion picture—was reported in the press. Money, money, money. It was fun to have the manager at the bank say "Good morning Mr. Crichton." But Bob had no interest in the power of money, only the freedom that it brought.

I'd never known anyone less interested in things. He wanted books and booze and time. Yes, we'd gone on one great shopping spree but there would never be another like it. He explained to the children that as we had once been broke but never poor, so we now had money but were not rich. The children found their situation confusing but understood.

Polishing his shoes one night with a kit that he had owned since boyhood, Bob reminded me that we were good people, decent people, honorable people who would not be corrupted by the trappings of success. He quoted from *The Lost Generation*, a book about the Americans who had gone off to Paris in the 1920s and '30s and produced sad, neurotic children, emotionally under-nourished, victim to self-centered parents and erratic childhoods. He would not let that happen to our birds who were now eight, ten, eleven and twelve. We would go out less, most of the parties we attended in the future would be in our own house, and the children would be with us.

I have four scrapbooks filled with clippings about *Santa Vittoria*. Mixed in with the reviews, interviews, and full-page ads is a playbill and a few reviews for a benefit held at Lincoln Center on November 6th, 1966: *Jerome Kern's Theater*. The following morning, *The New York Times* reported that "The show blended song, narration, and visual nostalgia (through marvelous slides of old programs, popular entertainers of the 1920s projected on a huge screen at the back of the stage) into such an unforgettable evening that one hardly knows how to begin dispensing the bravos. To the singers first . . . And then to Judy Crichton who wrote the effective script."

Curious the impact of one word: "effective." *Effective* is not a great word, not the kind of word one rolls around on the tongue—later, I'd do better—but it was good enough. The show was the first in a series of elaborate Lincoln Center benefits that, although credited to my uncle Dick Rodgers, was actually produced by his son-in-law Hank Guettel. Dick received a standing ovation, but the work was Hank's and mine and Burt Shevelove's, our talented friend who directed the production.

During the performance, I stayed in the projection booth at the top of the hall. The cues were complicated—there were three projectors—and I was playing backup. From that curious vantage point, I knew early on that the evening was an enormous success. During intermission, carrying the sound of the applause in my head, I went out onto the unprotected roof of what is now Alice Tully Hall to sort through my feelings. Looking down at the lights on the fountain, at the opera house with its magnificent chandeliers and the great Chagall murals, I broke through a barrier of my own devising.

Long before I met Bob, I had spent my youth hovering at the edge of concentric circles of talent. My cousin Mary Rodgers, my wickedly funny darling cousin Mary, had written the score for *Once Upon a Mattress* when she was in her mid-twenties. Our friend Hal Prince had set out to become the most creative director-producer in the country and succeeded; he was about to open *Cabaret* that November. And Burt Shevelove, brilliant, lonely, clever, funny Burt who had made Mary's family his own and adopted me by extension, had written *A Funny Thing Happened on the Way to the Forum* with Larry Gelbart. Hal produced *Forum* and Steve Sondheim wrote the songs, and I had known them all forever. I went to their rehearsals and previews and openings, always at the edge, basking in excitement that was never my own.

Portrait by Richard Avedon taken at a fundraiser
for the American Friends Service Committee

But on the roof of Philharmonic Hall that night, while I knew that some of the best lines in my script were Burt's rewrites, I felt I had begun to pay my way into the house.

As Bob and I left the concert hall, he was taking bows on the book and I was taking bows on the script, and Bob was proud of me. I had no illusions about parity, but I was committed now to finding a way to honor the creative impulses that had been part of my interior life since childhood.

On November 13th, 1966, *Santa Vittoria* became the best-selling novel in the country, and I was commissioned to find a new place to live. Our marble-topped table at La Salle Street could not seat more than five of us at a time, the children needed more quiet room to study, and Bob and I longed for privacy, too. Unleashed and with money, I found one apartment after another. All were rejected. Bob hated elevator men who would mark his comings-and-goings and whose civility was based on the size of their Christmas tips. He hated the East Side: too homogeneous, too bourgeois and tidy. He did not want to live in a one-class neighborhood. Bob wanted space and had begun to loathe the city but rejected every alternative I suggested.

Then one weekday morning, I went to see a duplex in a brownstone on a dead-end street in the West 70s. The space was smaller than I'd imagined but skylights filtered light down onto a living room-dining room space fifty feet long, with twelve-foot ceilings: finally a room large enough for Bob to dance in. By five that afternoon, we had bought the entire house for $45,000.

Bob was self-conscious about the house. His Aunt Julia Collier from St. Louis called it our New York City townhouse mansion. It was in fact a rowhouse built in the 1880s, four stories tall with an unreconstructed basement and a boiler larger and older than God that was to play a quixotic role in our life. Bob wore the purchase of the house like an oversized coat. He went through the sale without rejoicing, sent his lawyer to the closing and let me write the checks. We paid $16,000 down and had a 5% mortgage. While the house was under renovation, Bob seldom went near the place —at least, that was what we had thought.

I later discovered that on a bitter winter day, he happened by the house on the dead-end street and found that the sidewalk had turned to ice and that the stoop's steps were impassable. Borrowing a pick and shovel from a neighboring super, he set out to clear the walk and the stoop. He was visibly freezing when one of the Scottish carpenters working on the renovation invited him into the house for a cup of tea. Bob had a great time touring the site, admiring the work, never admitting to the crew that he was the mysterious owner. Every time it snowed, he'd make his way back. By now he owned his own equipment. He would clear the walk and have his tea and by the time spring arrived and we were finally able to move in, Bob and the carpenters were friends.

Bob on the stoop of what his Aunt Julia called
"your New York City townhouse mansion"

Bob and I both presumed that *Santa Vittoria's* success would give him the confidence he needed to move on with greater ease. But in some ways, the pressure seemed to have increased. Every reporter, every friend asked him what was next. He wasn't sure. Maybe the War Book, or maybe a fictionalized account of the Crichtons. He was increasingly obsessed with news from Vietnam and our systematic bombing of North Vietnam. In a letter to a friend he wrote:

> Someday when I see you I would like to explain the real secret reason for the device of the original manuscript for *Santa Vittoria* . . . I would have had to drop out that bombing sequence and with Viet Nam going on, I wasn't about to do that. The horror of the two chapters, of course, is the aimless way men will kill each other . . . the nothing of it, no passion on either side. Always in the name of honor, loyalty, country, service, obedience etc. All the abstract words we have been trained to honor.

In 1967, with the war escalating, Bob agreed to contribute an essay to a collection called *Authors Take Sides on Vietnam.* Bob's piece was short and horrific. It was principally a catalogue of the instruments the military was using on the people of Vietnam:

Napalm or jellied gasoline delivered in aluminum tanks triggered by white phosphorus bombs. On impact the bomb explodes and the now flaming gasoline consumes everything it comes in contact with. The effect on flesh is similar to that of a blowtorch or flamethrower but more tenacious. Nothing is wasted. Fragments of the phosphorus bomb itself, if they penetrate the body, will not stop burning for days, even after death, even in the grave.

Bob wrote about bombers setting off fire storms that covered thirty square miles, storms in which the heat rose to thousands of degrees and concluded saying that, "And perhaps for a nation with the burden of a Hiroshima or Nagasaki already to bear, this burning might become unbearable and something will go out of America that will never return."

In March of 1967 a telegram arrived addressed to The Young Crichtons.

Be kind to your father. Stop. As of this coming Sunday he is only number two. Stop. Tell him he must try harder. Gottlieb

That month, after fifteen years, *I've Got a Secret* went off the air.

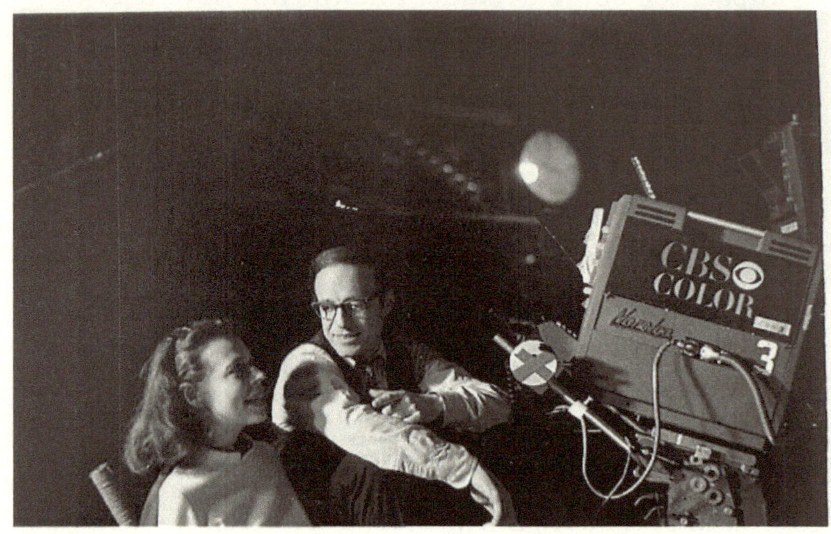

*On the I've Got a Secret set with
my work partner, Chester Feldman*

CHAPTER 22

I have come to think of the years surrounding *Santa Vittoria* as a period of unalloyed joy. There isn't such a time, of course, in anybody's life, and our first trip out of the United States together had its unsettling moments. *Santa Vittoria* had been published in England and was an enormous success. Bob was flown over for a publicity tour and, thanks to the generosity of the British publisher, I went with him. But the trip wasn't easy. We didn't know how to travel together. Since Suzy was born, we had spent only five days away from the children. We had so little practice.

Now Bob was famous and we moved around our large suite in Brown's Hotel like two actors in a play unsure of their lines. I reveled in the luxury of staying in one of the fine hotels of the world but Bob sank into a puritanical guilt-ridden funk. The sitting room with its blazing fireplace and antique furniture, the armoire for our clothes, the warming rack for the bath towels, the soap that stayed redolent, the bowls of fresh flowers—none of this was enough to dispel Bob's irritation. In fact, all of it probably contributed to his irritation.

But the children, from our apartment on La Salle Street where they were under the care of our housekeeper Ethel, wrote wonderful letters which we read over tea. I re-read them whenever I lost my way.

Sarah reported,

I'm memorizing The Love Song of J. Alfred Prudock [sic] by T.S. Eliot only it's 136 lines and Mr. Percival's making me memorize it all!

Ann Pleshette had her ears pierced the other day and if Rebecca of Sunnybrook farm had pierced ears she would look exactly like Ann. But I'm not really envious of Anny, Ellen or Debby 'cause if you look at older women they really look ridiculous and their ears sag which is quite normal of course but the whole (sic) in their ears really looks awful.

I wanted to call and tell Sarah it was all right. My mother had dismissed pierced ears, along with the anklet bracelet I so coveted when I was young. I had passed down too many of my mother's proscriptions, nonsense rules given weight like God's word, hounding one generation into the next, fueled by a terror of appearing vulgar.

But Rob wrote that "Ethel and we are all calm and peaceful." In a series of postscripts Sarah told us she'd signed up for the Gym Show, the rings, buck and horizontal bars, and then reported on her sister:

Do you know what Jenny did? She announced in assembly that all the fourth and fifth graders are invited to our house after Field Day. She's got to be cuckoo to invite 180 kids to our new clean house. That's all I can say. And finally, Pop, please tell me exactly what you feel about my reading *Moby Dick* this year be explicit please.

Bob was very proud of our birds. We relaxed together and enjoyed our tea.

The following morning we left the warmth of the hotel with a publicist named Michael, driving down to Portsmouth for a newspaper interview and a television appearance. Reaching the first appointment a half hour late, Bob and Michael scrambled, leaving me inside the car to explain to any bobby who happened by, why we'd been forced to park in a no-parking zone.

I sat in that car too long, too cold. By the time Bob returned, I was awash with fury, victim wife, self-conscious and angry. Bob offered no explanation. The presence of Michael, the press agent, a sweet chatty-Cathy doll of a man, imposed silence on us both and chaperoned our emotions.

Back in London, at Brown's Hotel, with a fire going and a proper bath and warmed towels, I managed to dress, and with that dreadful distance still between us, I picked up the heavy engraved invitation for the reception at New Zealand House, where Bob was to be honored with the other bestselling authors of the year.

As we walked into the reception, a butler announced Mr. and Mrs. Robert Crichton. I fluctuated in those days between taking pride in being Mrs. Robert Crichton and a desire for change. If you woke me in the middle of the night and asked "Who are you?", I would have said Bob's wife, the children's mother, the dog's keeper, my father's daughter. I had begun to turn myself into myself but I had yet to turn the corner. But I never did like being "Mrs. Robert Crichton" and disappearing altogether.

There were several hundred people in the room including a vicar who had written the definitive encyclopedia on wildflowers. I talked to the McWhirter brothers who had started the *Guinness Book of World Records*. The McWhirters and I had met before when I booked them on *I've Got a Secret*. They remembered and were gently pleased to see me. When we ran out of small talk, which did not take long, I drifted over to Bob who was talking to writer Nicholas Monsarrat, a courtly man known for his novels based on his wartime experience with the Royal Navy. I tried to match their animation but sensing I had failed, I drifted off again to stand by the wall of windows that looked over the city I had yet to really see.

It was there that Sir Harold Macmillan found me. I had no idea who he was, though his face was familiar, particularly the mustache. In 1967 I knew nothing about Macmillan. I'm not sure I even knew he'd been Prime Minister. My life was so crowded, English political literacy was not on my required list of study. And we were not introduced this evening.

"Do you know London?" Macmillan asked.

"I've never been here before."

"And what have you seen since your arrival?"

"Brown's Hotel," I answered. Not accurate but true enough.

"Ah, then," he said, "I'll take you on a tour."

I later learned that early in their marriage, Macmillan's wife began a life-long liaison with a bisexual scoundrel who had fathered Macmillan's youngest child. Now all I knew was that he was a kind and generous man on an evening when I was frightened and angry, and in a troubled marriage of my own. Macmillan started our tour in one corner of the room, and escorted me on our tour one window at a time, 360 degrees, around New Zealand House.

We began with King Alfred about whom I knew less than nothing, although Macmillan presumed I knew the basics. He moved down the catalogue of kings and described the creation of the city. He spoke of wars, of politics and architecture, and pointed out spires I could barely see. I loved the tour and was taken with this charming older man who seemed to be taken with me.

That I had not caught his name and that he didn't know mine was a matter of only modest concern. I was sorry when a young man who was clearly his aide broke up our tête-à-tête by suggesting that Sir Harold needed to move on. Macmillan took my hand and said, "I hope you have a happier time in London."

I thanked him for his courtesy, we both hesitated a moment, and then he was gone. A biography reported that Macmillan never had another romantic partner and lived a lonely life. But I suspect he had a talent for loving.

The moment of respite Macmillan's tour of London and English history had provided let me set my anger at Bob to the side. I was able to ask Bob quietly, without the furious tone I would have used earlier on, "Why did you abandon me this morning?"

"I forgot," he said.

Bob was gone long before he died. During the last months of his life, there was no flicker of recognition and then on March 23, 1993, he simply gave up breathing. He was 68 years old. We waited three months for the autopsy report, the final diagnosis from a neuropathologist at the Albert Einstein College of Medicine. When the report arrived, it transformed my thinking about Bob's life, and about our life together.

> We have completed the neuropathologic studies
> on your late husband, Robert C. Crichton, and
> have made a diagnosis of Pick's disease based on
> the presence of lobar atrophy and numerous Pick
> bodies found throughout the brain. The disease is
> quite rare. Your husband had no evidence of
> Wernicke-Korsakoff's disease, or other central
> nervous system pathology related to alcohol use.
> The clinical symptoms of Korsakoff's disease may
> overlap with those of Pick's disease.

No evidence of pathology related to alcohol use. No evidence. We were so wrong. For how many years did Bob, did I, did our friends, did my Aunt Dorothy blame all Bob's troubles on drinking? "Dear Judy," Bob had written, "I'll throw away my gin bottle to please you although the fault really isn't there but inside me. Just tell me to stop being so miserable inside and maybe I will control it."

Bob's life was erased slowly. After Bob died, Stuart Bartle sent me a chapter from a book on neurological disorders.

> The degenerative disorders usually begin insidiously and run a gradually progressive course over many years. The earliest changes may be so subtle that it often is impossible to assign any precise time of onset and are characterized by gradually evolving, relentlessly progressive neuronal death.

Bob must have sensed that controlling it—whatever the *it* was—was beyond his reach. His synapses were being strangled, the neurons were dying, the major circuits in his brain were being disrupted. When Bob's memory first began to slide, he was so clever, so fanciful, covering his tracks with Crichtonesque inventions as he had always done. Bob often swept us along, breathing magic into the commonplace.

But even early on there were moments that were too exaggerated, that pathology seemed to take over. That was the heart of the dilemma: Bob the wonderful storyteller who pushed at the edge of life and drew us along with him was also Bob the man who sometimes went too far and couldn't stop himself when he did. Over time, the magic of the storytelling seeped away. His inventive tales were no longer so entertaining but often as irritating as a child's bad joke told over and over, as when he came home with a story of a Great Dane that mistook his leg for a tree.

And he could no longer remember what he knew he had forgotten; he forgot he needed to cover his tracks. We watched as the tall and broad, friendly, talkative man who had walked in the glow of his own assurance and charm ended too many sentences midway with a sudden vacant look and "I can't remember."

Balance was lost one night on the Jersey Turnpike when Bob forgot how to drive and we were nearly killed. Rob had to do the unthinkable and order his father to stop the car, relinquish the keys and let him drive home. It was Rob's first time driving on a highway at night. At the time, it was so clear that Bob's drinking was to blame.

But it was not his fault. Wake him up from the dead, he did not die a drunk. For years Bob had been obsessed with the fear of non-being. His fears were rooted in the reality of the relentlessly progressive neuronal death but none of us knew or even suspected.

The magazines in the 1970s were filled with articles on how to shock alcoholics into quitting drinking. It was the age of the intervention. Bob sat at the head of the dining room table at 71st Street, surrounded by his birds, full grown but frightened, loving and angry.

"Pop, we want you around to see our children," Sarah said. We went around the table telling terrible Bob/Pop stories, talking about him as though he wasn't there. We hoped if only he could stop drinking, his brain would respond to what our doctor called the tincture of time.

So when Bob first went away, in the early 1980s to Spring Lake Ranch in Vermont, it was to dry out. A few months, half a year: that was his expected tenure there. Among their other sweet forms of therapy, the Spring Lake staff formed a book group and asked Bob to read from *The Secret of Santa Vittoria*.

"Read us your book," they asked.

"What book?" he asked. "Did I write a book?"

The months became a year at Spring Lake Ranch. Towards the end of his stay there, when common sense was all but gone and Bob could no longer care for himself, the Ranch called to say that Bob was missing. It was not the first time he had wandered off, but he had always come back before mealtime. As the hours passed, the State Police reported sightings of a tall lean man in khaki trousers walking on the side of the highway, headed east.

Late in the afternoon, a monk from a Catholic sanctuary phoned Spring Lake to say that Bob had wandered into his community, 25 miles away. Like a homing pigeon, Bob had been drawn to a Benedictine monastery (as his prep school, Portsmouth Priory, had been) devoted to protecting leftist exiles from Central America.

How had Bob learned of the sanctuary's existence? In that fog which all but obscured the world from his view, Bob had managed to make his way down the highway and the maze of back country roads to find what he'd always been seeking: one lovely place of religion, justice, love, music, peace. Even in the worst of days, there were these wondrous mysteries.

Suzy asked if it was her fault Pop needed to be institutionalized, if she had driven her father crazy. Oh Suzy! Suzy turned out to be one of the loveliest human beings God ever made. I looked at her and wondered if after she was born it was I who had tipped the psychic balance in the family, if it was my distraction and inattentiveness to the others, to Bob, to Sarah and Rob, and particularly Jen, that later fueled so many troubled feelings.

When Bob's cognitive and emotional state did not improve after he stopped drinking at Spring Lake Ranch, and in fact appeared to decline, doctors speculated that he was suffering from Wernicke-Korsakoff syndrome, a diminishment of brain volume and cognitive powers brought about by chronic drinking. A year passed and it was clear Bob needed to go elsewhere—first, a VA hospital in Westchester and then a fine-yet-grim nursing home nearby where he and one other broad-shouldered man stood heads and shoulders above the withered sparrow-like old people in the locked dementia ward.

During the last years of Bob's life and for some time following his death, I could not conjure him whole. I would call up his image and see him in the nursing home: the Bob who was not Bob. Over and over, Bob had written that the loss of memory murders life. But there are also memories that kill life and need to be suppressed.

Sarah said it best: "With Pop's death we have a chance of getting him back." We could remember Bob whole again.

On a rare sunny morning on Bainbridge Island, off the coast of Seattle, on a visit to Rob and his family, I looked up to find Rob seasoning his son Gillon's baseball mitt using a can of Neetfoot oil that his father had used on Rob's mitt many years before. And suddenly Bob began to re-emerge as the man he had been. Joy began to balance sadness. The grandchildren—there are five—began to hear Big Bob Crichton stories from their parents, from Bob's friends, from the Yemenites at the candy store a block away from our house on 71st Street. "Your grandfather was a giant of a man," Muhammed told them.

I went on to make another life, an interesting career and a partnership with a generous man who never tried to crowd Bob from my mind. Suzy died in 1995, two years after Bob. She spoke at his memorial service, telling the audience at the Harvard Club, "Of all the people who knew Pop and were affected by him, there are so many more who knew and loved him who we will never know." Of course, Suzy could be counted on to see and speak the truth. She lived longer than the time she'd been allotted but far shorter than we'd hoped.

There's a photo on my desk of Suzy and Bob together on a beach. He is thin yet broad, so tall that Suzy doesn't reach his waist. She looks up, small round person with a snub nose and searching look. It's not easy for them to connect; there's a host of differences between them. But thanks to those differences or in spite of them, Bob and Suzy connect, together on the shore.

*Bob and Judy with Philip Roth in Connecticut,
late 1970s (photo by Barbara Sproul)*

My mother Judy worked on "my book about Bob" for years, from the mid-1990s until she died in 2007. When my father died in 1993, it was finally clear he would not be coming back to the "big blue tomb" on 71st Street. My mother had to come to terms with those file cabinets in his office, stuffed to the gills with more than one lifetime of book and letter writing. And she wanted to make sense of this man whose presence still held sway in that office overlooking the quiet side street.

The memoir comes to a halt at the height of the *Santa Vittoria* success but at a moment, too, when my mother can glimpse the prospect of a rich and interesting career for herself. And she seems to realize that my father will never be able to meet her emotional needs.

In the years that followed, Judy became a documentary producer at CBS and ABC News: she took off. Pop wrote *The Camerons*, a wonderful novel drawn from his father's coalmining family in Scotland. *The Camerons* was a bestseller and its sale to paperback broke records. But the book didn't reach the dizzying heights that *Santa Vittoria* had. Pop busied himself in his office writing letters and funny postcards, chatted at length with the postman, and danced around his return to the War Book, the book he would finally write that became the book he would never finish.

Our mother began to travel for her work—fascinating, important travel to interview Castro in Cuba and leaders of the African National Congress in Zambia—and our father stayed home and lost his way.

After my mother died, her friend Barbara Masekela told me that the one thing Judy would have wanted was for someone to finish her book for her. I resisted for so long for so many reasons.

I can't speak specifically to Rob and Sarah's feelings about the book as our mother was working on it, but I think "mixed feelings" would apply to us all. For my part, Pop's decline, the sense of what he and we had lost, had been a core of my life since the late 1970s when his de-cline, depression and drinking took away the vibrant man we had known and loved. Sarah, Rob and I tracked and tried to obstruct or slow down this decline. It was clear to us; we saw him dissolve before our eyes.

More than fifteen years after my mother's death, though, I was ready to piece together her drafts. Guilt is my first language, and I knew I would not feel right if I came to the end of my own life with her manuscript lost to the limbo of a desk drawer. I could hear her chiding me from wherever she is, probably inside my head: "When when when?" She ran out of time. But I still had time.

My sister Sarah, the great editor, encouraged me to edit the manuscript in a way that made the book as readable and as alive as possible. Judy's later drafts tended to replace specific language with more generic, "writerly" choices. But as every writing teacher and editor knows, the specific language and details are where a story comes alive, and I always opted for her most specific iterations.

Judy showed her manuscript to many people along the way. She wrote to Stuart Bartle that "I would call it *Portrait of a Marriage,* if I had my druthers, but that title is already taken." A book by that name had come out in 1980. I think that after forty years, we can let Judy have the title she wanted.

This is Judy's story and in editing her drafts, I have tried not to put my finger on the scale to shape the book to my perspective. But I will add two points here to widen the context a bit. For all the complexity of the life that continued after the success of *Santa Vittoria* and Judy's work as a documentary producer that took her far afield from 71st Street, my parents were still a couple who loved each other, could have fun together, and nurtured a rich social life together. I was there and it was real—until it became too difficult in the early 1980s.

Pop and Sam on the 71st Street stoop

This portrait of a marriage would not be complete without mentioning Sam, the little dog who would not let Bob and Judy argue, but stood between them until they both laughed and backed down, who trotted alongside Pop on her way to Riverside Park, the plume of her tail waving with contented panache. When Sam died, Pop's deterioration sped up. Without Sam, he crashed.

When my father was first institutionalized, in 1985, a financial advisor told Judy to declare herself separated from him to avoid being sunk by the costs of his care. Judy had long been the financial manager for the family, a responsibility that she performed well. As this memoir made clear, she would not willingly invite poverty into her life, nor did she want her children to be burdened with her care when she was old.

As a result, Judy rarely visited Bob at the institutions he moved through: first Spring Lake Ranch ("saps collecting sap," he said of that community's enterprise making maple syrup); then a VA hospital in Westchester where his beautiful tweed jackets were stolen almost immediately; and finally the New Rochelle nursing home where he stood silent and broad among the shrunken assembly in the dementia unit. He died in March 1993 at the age of 68.

Our mother began a happy, less fraught relationship with Sandy Katz, a leftist public defender who had represented Black Panthers and loved to smoke and drink, fulminate about politics, and spend time in the small East Hampton house he had rented for years before our mother bought it for them.

Sandy may not have been my favorite dinner partner but he and Judy forged a genuine life together. For the first time in her life—literally—she traveled for pleasure. She and Sandy flew by Air France to Europe when it was the last air carrier to permit smoking on trans-Atlantic flights. She developed an active, happy social life in East Hampton with a core of his old friends.

In the spring of 2001, Sandy's doctor told him, not for the first time, "If you don't stop smoking and drinking, you're going to suffer a massive stroke." A week later, Sandy suffered that massive stroke and was wheelchair-bound for the rest of his life. My mother turned her energies to his care, and moved from the house on 71st Street to a sunny apartment on Broadway with the doormen my father always disdained. She loved that the doormen knew all her comings and goings—exactly what Pop had feared.

Then Sandy died in 2005 and Judy was diagnosed with leukemia a few months later. Her blood was almost all leukemic blast. Even if you don't know much about leukemia, *leukemic blast* says it all. Sarah and I were with her when the oncologist explained the situation. Sarah, Mom and I all whipped out our notebooks in exactly the same way at exactly the same moment, a choreography of instilled family culture. To write is to take control.

"Put those notebooks away for now," the doctor said firmly, kindly. Even without our notebooks, we managed to hear and grasp what she had to say.

The leukemia was very far gone. But there was an experimental protocol designed for older patients like Judy. It had been successful in only a tiny percentage of the study's participants, and we would know in a month or two if Judy was one of the lucky ones.

"And if I'm not?" she asked.

"Then we make you as comfortable as possible."

We were all lucky that the experimental protocol—a grueling haul of chemotherapy taken not by drip but by a capsule three times a week, as brutal for her as any chemotherapy given to anyone I have known—brought her to the other side. For a time, she was well, with a wonderful silvery cap of sleek curls that emerged out of the sea change of chemotherapy.

We all went to Cape Cod together the summer she recovered: Rob, Sarah and I, and all our kids. Then, in September, Judy had her dream wish and took Gillon to Banana Republic to outfit him for his first year of college.

Most important, we all had the conversations with her we needed to have, sometimes long and hard, sometimes brief and vibrating with love. And she worked on this book, tracing the past and searching for where and when Bob had disappeared.

Was the cause of Bob "losing his mind" only drinking? To our mother, that question seemed critical. To my mind, the reality of the decline itself was the most important thing. If drinking was the prime mover, was that still considered a moral failure? Did that make it his fault? But for Judy, the revelation of the Pick's disease diagnosis released Bob from the guilt of having brought on dementia by his drinking. "Wake him up from the dead, he did not die a drunk," she wrote in her epilogue.

When Pop died, the Pick's disease diagnosis seemed definitive. But I am less convinced that Pick's disease was the sole cause of his cognitive decline. Pick's symptoms are identical to other forms of frontal-temporal dementia, including CTE (chronic traumatic encephalopathy) caused by concussion and other brain injury. When our father died in 1993, CTE was not even among the brain disorders searched for in the autopsy.

But this is Judy's story and her goal in telling it was, in part, to trace where Bob's decline began. The impulsivity and mood swings of his earlier years: Were they the precursors of the dementia to follow? That question was not the only one she wanted to explore in this book, but it is one that led her through the story of the life she and my father shared. And it's a question she seemed to feel had been answered, at least in part.

In pulling together my mother's memoir, I loved spending time with Mom and Pop and Suzy after all these years. Suzy: the one person in my life before I had my own children who loved me unconditionally and, in so doing, taught me how to love. As I write this, my heart floods with love for Suzy and for my brother and sister, Rob and Sarah. We didn't have an easy time of it. For Suzy, none of it was ever easy. But we have done our best to love those in our life. Mom and Pop would be proud of their birds.

Special thanks to Jeri Laber, my mother's great friend, for reading an almost-finished draft and providing important insights, as well as spotting spelling and grammar mistakes so elusive to one's own eye. And special thanks to my daughter, Catherine Emil. I hate to strengthen the trope that millennials are whizzes at tech and boomers are bumbling doofuses. But Cat helped me with critical lay-out issues—while I managed everything else. That hour or two of help, and her encouraging words, made all the difference.

Catherine and my brother Rob then trained their eagle eyes on the many typos and format glitches still remaining in the first press run of this book. Many thanks to them for being the sticklers they are. Thanks too to my sister Sarah for her guidance and support, and David Emil for not insisting I include the story of how my mother chose him as my husband when I was eleven years old. That will have to wait for another time.

As much as she struggled with our father's myth-making, Judy could be dogged about defending her illusions, too.

"Do you smoke?" asked the oncologist at that first visit.

"Yes."

"Since she was 15," Sarah said.

"But if I have leukemia, it's not because of smoking," our mother said quickly. "It's because I was exposed to radiation at Three Mile Island."

"You were at Three Mile Island?"

"Yes, I'm a journalist." Proud. Proudly exposed to radioactivity.

What caused her leukemia? Was it sixty years of smoking or a few days' exposure to radioactivity at Three Mile Island?

This is Judy's book, her life, her story. Leukemia was her diagnosis. Who really knows about these diagnoses and these causes, anyway? Three Mile Island, it is.

Jennifer Crichton
Burlington, Vermont
February 2024

Judy Crichton was among the first women to write, direct and produce documentaries at the CBS and ABC news divisions in the 1970s. Among her many works, she was most proud of "The CIA's Secret Army," which revealed the terrorist activities of Cuban exiles in Miami and the support they received from the CIA, and "The Battle for South Africa," one of the first US reports to interview future South Africa president, Thabo Mbeki.

In the 1980s, Crichton became founding executive producer of *American Experience*, the PBS history series. During her tenure, the series won seven Emmys; six Peabody Awards; five Writers Guild Awards; and two Alfred I. duPont-Columbia Journalism Awards. In 1998, Judy Crichton received the Writers Guild's Evelyn F. Burkey Award, a lifetime achievement award presented annually to a television writer.

When Crichton was elected a member of the Society of American Historians, she was one of the few inductees with the singular distinction of having never attended college, learned a language other than English, or published in an academic journal. But as President Bill Clinton said in 2000 when he awarded her the National Humanities Medal, "In creating and producing *American Experience*, she set a new standard for what television documentaries can be. With talent, passion and purpose, Judy Crichton has elevated a medium she loves and lifted all those who watch it."

Crichton's first book was *1900: The Turning Point* (Holt 1998). She died in 2007 at the age of 77.

www.ingramcontent.com/pod-product-compliance
Lightning Source LLC
Chambersburg PA
CBHW031444160726
47994CB00005B/1864